Oct 21

OPPOSING VIEWPOINTS® SERIES

Racial Discrimination and Criminal Justice

Other Books of Related Interest

Opposing Viewpoints Series

America's Changing Demographics
Feminism
Gender in the 21st Century
Interpreting the Bill of Rights
Toxic Masculinity

At Issue Series

Civil Disobedience
Cyberwarfare
The Federal Budget and Government Spending
Gender Politics
The Opioid Crisis

Current Controversies Series

America's Mental Health Crisis
Are There Two Americas?
Drones, Surveillance, and Targeted Killings
Enhanced Interrogation and Torture
Returning Soldiers and PTSD

"Congress shall make no law ... abridging the freedom of speech, or of the press."

The basic foundation of our democracy is the First Amendment guarantee of freedom of expression. The Opposing Viewpoints series is dedicated to the concept of this basic freedom and the idea that it is more important to practice it than to enshrine it.

Racial Discrimination and Criminal Justice

Martin Gitlin, Book Editor

GREENHAVEN
PUBLISHING

Published in 2022 by Greenhaven Publishing, LLC
353 3rd Avenue, Suite 255, New York, NY 10010

Articles in Greenhaven Publishing anthologies are often edited for length to meet page
requirements. In addition, original titles of these works are changed to clearly present
the main thesis and to explicitly indicate the author's opinion. Every effort is made to
ensure that Greenhaven Publishing accurately reflects the original intent of the authors.
Every effort has been made to trace the owners of the copyrighted material.

Cover image: AlessandroBiascioli/Shutterstock.com

Library of Congress Cataloging-in-Publication Data
Names: Gitlin, Marty, editor.
Title: Racial discrimination and criminal justice / Martin Gitlin, book
    editor.
Description: First edition. | New York, NY : Greenhaven Publishing, LLC,
    2022. | Series: Opposing viewpoints | Includes bibliographical
    references and index. | Contents: Is racial discrimination a police
    problem? — Is the court system biased against people of color? — Would
    changing laws change outcomes? — A gaze into the future | Audience: Ages 15+
    | Audience: Grades 10–12 | Summary: "The viewpoints
    in this volume examine the truths regarding the justice system and
    people of color in the United States. Experts from the field offer very different
    perspectives on this important topic"— Provided by publisher.
Identifiers: LCCN 2020051603 | ISBN 9781534507715 (library binding) | ISBN
    9781534507692 (paperback)
Subjects: LCSH: Discrimination in criminal justice administration—United
    States.
Classification: LCC KF9223 .R33 2022 | DDC 364.3/400973—dc23
LC record available at https://lccn.loc.gov/2020051603

Manufactured in the United States of America

Website: http://greenhavenpublishing.com

Contents

Chapter 4: What Is the Future of Criminal Justice in America?

The Importance of Opposing Viewpoints

Perhaps every generation experiences a period in time in which the populace seems especially polarized, starkly divided on the important issues of the day and gravitating toward the far ends of the political spectrum and away from a consensus-facilitating middle ground. The world that today's students are growing up in and that they will soon enter into as active and engaged citizens is deeply fragmented in just this way. Issues relating to terrorism, immigration, women's rights, minority rights, race relations, health care, taxation, wealth and poverty, the environment, policing, military intervention, the proper role of government—in some ways, perennial issues that are freshly and uniquely urgent and vital with each new generation—are currently roiling the world.

If we are to foster a knowledgeable, responsible, active, and engaged citizenry among today's youth, we must provide them with the intellectual, interpretive, and critical-thinking tools and experience necessary to make sense of the world around them and of the all-important debates and arguments that inform it. After all, the outcome of these debates will in large measure determine the future course, prospects, and outcomes of the world and its peoples, particularly its youth. If they are to become successful members of society and productive and informed citizens, students need to learn how to evaluate the strengths and weaknesses of someone else's arguments, how to sift fact from opinion and fallacy, and how to test the relative merits and validity of their own opinions against the known facts and the best possible available information. The landmark series Opposing Viewpoints has been providing students with just such critical-thinking skills and exposure to the debates surrounding society's most urgent contemporary issues for many years, and it continues to serve this essential role with undiminished commitment, care, and rigor.

The key to the series's success in achieving its goal of sharpening students' critical-thinking and analytic skills resides in its title—

Opposing Viewpoints. In every intriguing, compelling, and engaging volume of this series, readers are presented with the widest possible spectrum of distinct viewpoints, expert opinions, and informed argumentation and commentary, supplied by some of today's leading academics, thinkers, analysts, politicians, policy makers, economists, activists, change agents, and advocates. Every opinion and argument anthologized here is presented objectively and accorded respect. There is no editorializing in any introductory text or in the arrangement and order of the pieces. No piece is included as a "straw man," an easy ideological target for cheap point-scoring. As wide and inclusive a range of viewpoints as possible is offered, with no privileging of one particular political ideology or cultural perspective over another. It is left to each individual reader to evaluate the relative merits of each argument—as he or she sees it, and with the use of ever-growing critical-thinking skills—and grapple with his or her own assumptions, beliefs, and perspectives to determine how convincing or successful any given argument is and how the reader's own stance on the issue may be modified or altered in response to it.

This process is facilitated and supported by volume, chapter, and selection introductions that provide readers with the essential context they need to begin engaging with the spotlighted issues, with the debates surrounding them, and with their own perhaps shifting or nascent opinions on them. In addition, guided reading and discussion questions encourage readers to determine the authors' point of view and purpose, interrogate and analyze the various arguments and their rhetoric and structure, evaluate the arguments' strengths and weaknesses, test their claims against available facts and evidence, judge the validity of the reasoning, and bring into clearer, sharper focus the reader's own beliefs and conclusions and how they may differ from or align with those in the collection or those of their classmates.

Research has shown that reading comprehension skills improve dramatically when students are provided with compelling, intriguing, and relevant "discussable" texts. The subject matter of these collections could not be more compelling, intriguing, or urgently relevant to today's students and the world they are poised to inherit. The anthologized articles and the reading and discussion questions that are included with them also provide the basis for stimulating, lively, and passionate classroom debates. Students who are compelled to anticipate objections to their own argument and identify the flaws in those of an opponent read more carefully, think more critically, and steep themselves in relevant context, facts, and information more thoroughly. In short, using discussable text of the kind provided by every single volume in the Opposing Viewpoints series encourages close reading, facilitates reading comprehension, fosters research, strengthens critical thinking, and greatly enlivens and energizes classroom discussion and participation. The entire learning process is deepened, extended, and strengthened.

For all of these reasons, Opposing Viewpoints continues to be exactly the right resource at exactly the right time—when we most need to provide readers with the critical-thinking tools and skills that will not only serve them well in school but also in their careers and their daily lives as decision-making family members, community members, and citizens. This series encourages respectful engagement with and analysis of opposing viewpoints and fosters a resulting increase in the strength and rigor of one's own opinions and stances. As such, it helps make readers "future ready," and that readiness will pay rich dividends for the readers themselves, for the citizenry, for our society, and for the world at large.

Introduction

> *"Mass imprisonment has littered the national landscape with carceral monuments of reckless and excessive punishment and ravaged communities with our hopeless willingness to condemn and discard the most vulnerable among us."*
>
> —*Bryan Stevenson,* Just Mercy: A Story of Justice and Redemption

The problem of racial discrimination is so wide-ranging and pervasive that, to millions of people, it has become the most critical issue facing the United States. It is believed strongly that America cannot live out its creed that all people are created equal if the country does not successfully work to ensure racial equality in all areas of society.

Issues regarding discrimination in the court system and violence at the hands of law enforcement had been firmly in the shadows before technology changed everything. Footage recorded by cell phone cameras and body cameras revealed harrowing acts of police brutality for all to see. The proliferation of social media ushered in an explosion of passionate opinions about the injustices that Americans of color face from our justice system. Almost suddenly, all matters of racial discrimination and criminal justice reform were placed squarely in the spotlight.

And just as one spotlight shines on the maltreatment of people of color by police and security officers for such lawful activities as driving in white neighborhoods or shopping in upscale stores, another spotlight rests upon white people who enjoy the privilege of being born with a luckier skin color. Millions of Americans of all shades believe that not only is the vast income gap between black and white a reflection of racial discrimination but so is the way all races are viewed in the eyes of law enforcement and the halls of justice.

The most shocking of all visuals, one that has motivated protests of all sizes in communities throughout the country, have been the highly publicized shootings and often killings of unarmed Black men and women by police. One after another, they were seen on televisions and computer screens by hundreds of millions around the world, convincing people outside the country that the United States was a nation in chaos. Perhaps the most impactful was the 2020 police killing of George Floyd during an arrest in Minneapolis. Outrage from this injustice compelled more than 10,000 demonstrations around the United States in the months following Floyd's death. While the majority of protests were peaceful, some devolved into riots and looting, acts that fueled detractors' prejudice.

Most viewed the deadly confrontations between police and people of color as proof of at least mild if not rampant racism in American law enforcement. Even the majority of police departments acknowledge the problem. But solving racism in the criminal justice system is a massive undertaking. Every road seems fraught with danger. Cries to "defund the police," suggesting a change in the response to activity that traditionally would be the purview of the police, seemed frightening and overwhelming. For instance, if money is diverted from the police to social services, how can officers patrol the streets effectively when gang warfare is killing thousands every year?

Many cops have asked critics to walk a mile in their shoes. They argue that they are overworked and understaffed, and that their very dangerous job often requires they make quick life-or-death decisions. The counterpoint is that citizens of all colors deserve the right to be treated with equal fairness and compassion. Attempts at nipping crime in the bud through stop-and-frisk laws failed greatly because young African Americans and Latinos were far more often perceived with suspicion than their white counterparts. The result was that innocent people were targeted simply because of the color of their skin. Politicians who had advocated stop-and-frisk policies were forced to apologize so they could keep their jobs in a more heated, racially charged political climate. But some still backed the concept of stop-and-frisk if it could be carried out without prejudice.

That ship had already sailed regarding the criminal justice system. Statistics proved time and again that for decades the courts had been meting out far stricter punishments to Black men than to their white counterparts for most crimes—from minor offenses all the way up to crimes that resulted in the death penalty. Even conservative Republicans recognized the imbalance, leading to criminal justice reform.

But the problem of mass incarceration of African Americans could hardly be solved through one legislative effort. Racism permeates throughout American society and leads to many unanswered questions. Why have people of color historically been given harsher sentences? Why do white collar criminals who bilk large sums of money receive more lenient punishment than poor people of color who commit petty thefts? How can US society work to stop young Black and Hispanic boys from feeling that joining gangs and committing violent crimes are the only tickets to a positive self-image? Must police departments hire more Black officers to patrol Black communities, or can the elimination of racism make that unnecessary? And would the addition of Black officers alone lessen crime rates?

Claims that racial profiling is limited to dangerous areas in which gangs commit mayhem seem to ignore the pleas of millions of Black people around the country. Even wealthy or well-known people of color have publicized stories of confrontations with police or white citizens. Perhaps they were pulled over simply for driving along in a predominantly white neighborhood. Perhaps they were followed around a store while shopping. Perhaps they were sitting in their own front yards and they were harassed by white neighbors who didn't believe that they owned their homes. Such confrontations have been commonplace for decades. But cell phone cameras and alert people on the streets have allowed all of America to understand that racial prejudice remains a huge problem.

Most Americans embrace the notion that all people are created equal. Recent events have proven more than ever that all people are not treated equal by fellow Americans, law enforcement, or the criminal justice system. And until they are, true equality in the United States will remain more a concept than an achieved reality.

The diverse perspectives contained in *Opposing Viewpoints: Racial Discrimination and Criminal Justice* confront America's criminal justice system through the lens of racial equality head-on in chapters titled "Is Racial Discrimination a Police Problem?"; "Is the Court System Biased Against People of Color?"; "Would Changing Laws Change Outcomes?"; and "What Is the Future of Criminal Justice in America?"

**OPPOSING
VIEWPOINTS®
SERIES**

CHAPTER 1

Is Racial Discrimination a Police Problem?

Chapter Preface

The relationship between American law enforcement and the African American community cannot be generalized. Every police department handles its job with different levels of competence and compassion. Every officer is a human being with different experiences, thoughts, and feelings. And there can be vast differences in the communities they police. An urban environment presents different challenges than a small town or a suburb.

But there is clearly a problem. Alarming statistics as well as video proof of highly publicized confrontations that often turn deadly indicate that some police officers treat Black citizens more harshly than their white counterparts. A spate of supposedly minor conflicts between law enforcement that escalated into the murders of young Black men inspired the Black Lives Matter movement. This blossomed into a wave of protests that for the first time in American history included a large percentage of white participants, many of whom understood for the first time what had been happening all along.

Such events shone a stronger spotlight on the relationship between police and African Americans, prompting a slew of questions. Were these murders a result of a few bad apples in specific police departments? Or were they proof of rampant systemic racism? Has such maltreatment been going on for decades and only been uncovered by the advent of cell phone and police body cameras? Has too much money and attention been paid to cracking down on inner city gangs and not enough on social services that will help those in poorer communities live better and more lawful lives? Has what many perceive as the "good old days" of community policing in which officers got to know and became friends with the people they served been destroyed forever? Or can it and should it be reinstated?

The viewpoints in this chapter will examine such issues revolving around the perceived targeting of African Americans by law enforcement and the results, as well as potential solutions to the problem.

"Black people are forced, by armed officers of the government, to justify their presence. They have the burden of proof; the person who called the police is assumed to be correct."

The Policing of Black Americans Is Racial Harassment Funded by the State

Paul Butler

In the following viewpoint, Paul Butler argues that the police's job is to uphold a racialized law and order. The author cites harassment of Black people by their fellow citizens and the resulting confrontations that have often turned deadly. Butler refers to the suspicion engendered by the mere sight of African Americans going about their everyday business that motivates calls to the police and the feelings of helplessness and anger that permeates within the victims. Paul Butler is a law professor at Georgetown University and an MSNBC legal analyst. He is a former federal prosecutor and the author of Chokehold: Policing Black Men.

As you read, consider the following questions:

1. Why does the author place more blame on the system than on police officers for maltreatment of African Americans?
2. What suggestions does the author make to improve relations between cops and residents of urban communities?
3. What does it mean to transform from "warrior" to "guardian" mentality?

The rap group Public Enemy famously stated that "911 is a joke." But that was in 1990. These days 911 is dead serious. Anyone in the United States can dial those three numbers and summon people with guns and handcuffs to participate in their anti-black paranoia. It's racial harassment, sponsored by the government and supported by tax dollars.

When one calls 911 in New York City, the first question the dispatcher asks is "What is your emergency?" I wonder how the white people recently in the news for calling the police on black folks would have answered that question. "Two men sitting at Starbucks." "Four women golfing slowly." "Graduate student napping." "Man moving into apartment." "Women moving luggage out of a house."

The people who call the police are not the main problem. Of course those people are, to use an old-fashioned word, prejudiced. It is difficult to imagine them being made anxious by white people going about the business of their everyday lives. But this kind of racism for black people is, in fact, everyday.

This does not mean that it is acceptable: everyday racism is aggravating, health draining, and, for its survivors, labor intensive. Everyday racism requires a performance when a black person navigates white spaces. You conspicuously display your work ID. You look down on the elevator. You whistle Vivaldi.

The people who call the police can fill a black person with a productive rage or a corrosive kind of hate. In my ideal world, when people call the police on black people for no good reason, they would be taken to a public place and beaten with sticks. By black people. They are spirit murderers. But still they are not the main problem.

The main problem is the response of the state. "We'll send a squad over right away." The caller has offered a short pitch for a white supremacist fantasia, and now the dispatcher green-lights it. She sends a crew over to the set identified by the caller and the spectacle is produced.

Black people are forced, by armed officers of the government, to justify their presence. They have the burden of proof; the person who called the police is assumed to be correct. That the black person gets to make her case at all is an incremental evolution in justice from the antebellum south, where white people could and did make all manner of false accusations against blacks but black people were not allowed to be witnesses against whites in any official proceeding.

In recent cases, black people have offered excuses like "golfing," "napping" and "moving." For two African American men at a Starbucks in Philadelphia, "waiting for a friend" is deemed insufficient. The men are placed in handcuffs and taken to jail. The Philadelphia police chief, Richard Ross, says "the police did absolutely nothing wrong." Later, when the arrests created a national firestorm, the chief apologizes. He says that, as a black man, he should have known better.

What I want to say is that usually the police know better, and it does not matter. Darren Martin had the police called on him when he was just moving into a new apartment in Manhattan. A neighbor claimed he was breaking down the door and had a weapon. Martin had the presence of mind, and courage, to livestream the police response.

The six NYPD officers who reported to the scene discovered a young black man moving stuff to a fifth-floor walk-up. Still the cops put Martin through the procedure, interrogating him and forcing him to show ID. When Martin protested, the officers stood there with a stupid look on their faces. It's the "we are just doing our jobs" expression.

The sad thing is that they are exactly right. Enforcing a racialized law and order is an important function of police work in the 21st century. In my book *Chokehold*, I suggest that the problem is not bad apple cops. The problem is the system is working the way it is supposed to. The US criminal legal process is all about keeping people—especially African American men—in their place. Even when trespassing white space is not an arrestable offense, it can occasion a fraught encounter.

The Harvard scholar Henry Louis Gates Jr wrote: "Black men swap their experiences of police encounters like war stories, and there are few who don't have more than one story to tell." The crazy thing is that Gates wrotes this in 1995, long before he was arrested by the Cambridge police after a neighbor called the police to report he was trespassing on his own front porch. I have more stories than I can count. The time the police followed me when I was walking in my neighborhood and told me to go in my house to prove that I lived there. The evening I worked late and the night security guard barged into my office and demanded my work ID. Afterwards the primary emotions are anger—no matter what you do you still get judged by the color of your skin—and relief—at least you got out of this one without being arrested, beat up, or killed.

The structure that allows this cannot stand. I make that claim hopefully, as when Martin Luther King Jr said: "the arc of the moral universe curves toward justice." I also make that claim descriptively, as when King said "no lie can live forever." In *Chokehold*, I suggest ways of improving relations between the police and communities of color, including having more women and college-educated cops, who the data suggests, respond to these kind of situations more effectively. Ultimately the whole culture of policing must be transformed, from the "warrior" mentality that Barack Obama described, to one of "guardians."

It turns out that, back in 1990, when Public Enemy described 911 as a joke, they weren't even talking about the police. Their complaint was that paramedics didn't show up when they were summoned to the hood. Those were the first responders who the community would have welcomed. Long before the viral videos of police abuse, many black folks had already given up on the cops.

> *"But why is Shopping While Black still a thing? According to a Nielsen report released last month, African-American buying power amounts to $1tn—yes, trillion—a year. This has everything to do with stereotyping and very little to do with reality."*

"Shopping While Black" Is Still an Issue

Teresa Wiltz

In the following viewpoint, Teresa Wiltz argues that dark skinned people are targeted and harassed while shopping in stores, a practice known as "retail racism." Even well-known and wealthy customers, such as Oprah Winfrey, have been discriminated against. Though the author places a spotlight on one particular store, she cites the experiences of other Black people who have suffered the same indignity while simply shopping to show further proof that the problem is significant and discriminatory. She cites statistics to prove her contentions that show that shoplifters come in all colors. Teresa Wiltz is a journalist who was a staff writer for the Washington Post *and* Chicago Tribune. *She is author of* The Real America.

"'Shopping While Black' Is Still an Issue—at Barneys and Elsewhere," by Teresa Wiltz, Guardian News & Media, October 28, 2013. Copyright Guardian News & Media Ltd. 2020. Reprinted by permission.

As you read, consider the following questions:

1. How do you define the issue of "Shopping While Black"?
2. How do examples of celebrities bolster claims that retail racism exists?
3. Why does the author mention actress Winona Ryder?

Y ou could say I grew up in Barneys.

When I was a little girl living in Staten Island, whenever my dad needed a new suit, we'd ferry it into Manhattan and head on over to Barneys. There, I'd spend many a happy hour playing in the racks while my dad tried on clothes. Scroll forward a few years: I'm in college and my dad and I are hanging in the city. Naturally, we head over to our favorite store for a little shopping/bonding excursion. I even remember what he bought for me that day: a rust-colored Norma Kamali one piece. (Hey, it was the '80s.) From those early days, I developed a taste for high-end clothes (thanks, Pops) and an abiding love for all things Barneys.

But now Barneys has a serious image problem.

Color me conflicted.

Hearing what allegedly happened to Trayon Christian, a young black engineering student, at their flagship store on Madison Avenue is the kind of thing that makes me want to huff and puff and blow the joint down. It's infuriating. Now, he's suing them—and I don't blame him. If Barney's really did call the cops on him simply for buying an expensive belt that the store assumed he could not afford, then something is serious wrong.

Barneys' image problem doesn't stop there: another African-American shopper has come forward to say that she, too, was racially profiled by cops while shopping there. There's an online petition demanding that Jay-Z, who is collaborating with them on a capsule clothing collection, to sever his ties with them. The petition crosses out "Barneys New York" and writes "Barneys New Slaves."

In a statement posted on his website over the weekend, Jay-Z said he was being "unfairly demonized" for waiting to hear the facts.

He said he would not be making a dime off of his collaboration with Barneys; proceeds would benefit his charity, the Shawn Carter Foundation. He also said he's no stranger to retail racism.

And now, the retailer, after initially denying the allegations, has hired a civil rights lawyer to review all aspects of the store's operations. To show how serious they are about having "zero tolerance for any form of discrimination," as they declared on their Facebook page, the store's CEO will reportedly meet with Reverend Al Sharpton and his National Action Network.

You know it's serious when Reverend Al gets called in for a huddle.

Now, you could dismiss the brouhaha as nothing more than a case of schadenfreude, watching one luxury retailer with a rep for snobbery take a tumble in the public eye.

But as Oprah Winfrey would be the first to tell you, this isn't about Barneys. Earlier this year, while shopping in Switzerland, she was rebuffed from buying a super pricey bag. This summer, two former "perfumistas" at Bond No. 9, a luxury perfume shop in Manhattan, sued the retailer for racial discrimination against employees and customers. Whenever African Americans entered the store, the suit alleges, employees were instructed to go on alert and use this key phrase: "the light bulbs need changing."

Yes, Shopping While Black is still a thing.

I have to say, I've always been treated just fine at Barneys. I wouldn't shop there if I wasn't. (And a good chunk of their staff is of color.) But I have been followed all over Lord & Taylor by a security guard squawking into her walkie talkie, tracking my whereabouts. When you're painted brown, a black Amex card can't protect you from a salesperson who takes one look at you and makes a judgment call about the state of your finances—and your ability to pay for whatever it is they're selling.

And sometimes, as was the case of the security guard at Lord & Taylor, the ones doing the judging are black and brown, too. Institutionalized racism is something that we've all internalized.

But why is Shopping While Black still a thing? According to a Nielsen report released last month, African-American buying power amounts to $1tn—yes, trillion—a year. This has everything to do with stereotyping and very little to do with reality.

And for those of you who insist that racial profiling is a necessary evil, the only practical means to combat shoplifting: save it. According to the National Association for Shoplifting Prevention, there is no profile for a typical shoplifter—they come in all colors and across all income brackets. Barneys should be the first to recognize this. Remember Winona Ryder?

"Police killings of unarmed black men were associated with an increase in mental health problems such as depression and emotional issues for black people living in the state where the killing took place."

Getting Killed by Police Is a Leading Cause of Death for Young Black Men in America

Amina Khan

In the following viewpoint, Amina Khan argues that Black men are particularly vulnerable and most likely to be killed in police custody. The author uses statistics to highlight police mistreatment of African Americans, as well as Latinos and Native Americans. She cites scientific studies to prove that confrontations with police have contributed to a higher rate of emotional and mental problems among Black men. Khan also quotes law enforcement officials that admit the problem of racial profiling and the need for officers and departments to make changes. Amina Khan is a science writer for the Los Angeles Times.

"Getting Killed by Police Is a Leading Cause of Death for Young Black Men in America," by Amina Khan, *Los Angeles Times*, August 16, 2019. Reprinted with permission.

As you read, consider the following questions:

1. How does the author use statistics to make her points?
2. Are psychological studies effective in enlightening readers about how violent police interactions affect people of color?
3. Does the author perceive strong cooperation among police departments across the country in acknowledging and changing policy and behavior?

About 1 in 1,000 black men and boys in America can expect to die at the hands of police, according to a new analysis of deaths involving law enforcement officers. That makes them 2.5 times more likely than white men and boys to die during an encounter with cops.

The analysis also showed that Latino men and boys, black women and girls and Native American men, women and children are also killed by police at higher rates than their white peers. But the vulnerability of black males was particularly striking.

"That 1-in-1,000 number struck us as quite high," said study leader Frank Edwards, a sociologist at Rutgers University. "That's better odds of being killed by police than you have of winning a lot of scratch-off lottery games."

The number-crunching by Edwards and his coauthors also revealed that for all young men, police violence was one of the leading causes of death in the years 2013 to 2018.

The Deadly Toll of Police Violence

A new study finds that about 1 in 1,000 black men and boys can expect to die as a result of police violence over the course of their lives—a risk that's about 2.5 times higher than their white peers. The annual risk rises and falls with age, and is highest for young men. Here's how it compares to other leading causes of death for black men in their mid-to-late 20s.

CAUSE OF DEATH	MORTALITY RATE*
Assault	94.2
Accidents	52.1
Suicide	17.5
Heart disease	14
HIV	6.8
Cancer	6.2
Police use of force**	3.4
Diabetes	2.8
Influenza and pneumonia	2
Chronic lower respiratory disease	2
Cerebrovascular diseases	1.9

*Annual mortality rates are reported as deaths per 100,000 black men ages 25 to 29.
**Figure is the median of 2013-2018 mortality rate calculated in PNAS study led by Frank Edwards.

Source: Centers for Disease Control and Prevention, 2015.

The findings, published this month in the *Proceedings of the National Academy of Sciences*, add hard numbers to a pattern personified by victims like Eric Garner, Tamir Rice and Freddie Gray.

Five years after police in the St. Louis suburb of Ferguson, Mo., fatally shot Michael Brown, protesters and activist groups have focused public attention on the disproportionate use of force against African Americans and other people of color.

Scientists, meanwhile, are increasingly studying police violence as a public health problem whose long-term harms radiate far beyond the original victim.

"It can have these toxic effects on communities, in terms of both their physical and mental health," Edwards said.

A study published in the *Lancet* last year found that police killings of unarmed black men were associated with an increase in mental health problems such as depression and emotional issues for black people living in the state where the killing took place.

And living in a state of constant fear can lead to chronic stress, Edwards said. He referred to "the talk," a conversation that many African American parents have with their children—especially boys—about how to interact with police to avoid being harmed.

"They know that young black men are singled out as being inherently suspect," he said.

Accurately measuring the mortality rate associated with police violence right alongside those of cancer, heart disease and other major causes of death is a crucial step toward mitigating its damage and even "treating" its root causes. But calculating the true rate of police killings is difficult because official data are limited, researchers said.

The National Vital Statistics System captures some of these deaths, but it appears to underreport them, researchers said. This might have to do with the information given to coroners and medical examiners, or with the way they code deaths; the researchers can't say for sure.

To pull those numbers together, Edwards and his colleagues turned to Fatal Encounters, a journalist-led system that collects and combines information on police violence that's available through news coverage, public records and social media. Although not an official database, it appears to provide comprehensive information on recent police killings and has been endorsed as a sound source of data by the federal government's Bureau of Justice Statistics, the researchers said.

By combining and then analyzing information from Fatal Encounters and the National Vital Statistics System, the team was able to calculate the prevalence of fatal police violence overall and according to race, age and gender. Cases that police described as suicides were excluded, as were those involving a vehicle collision or accident such as an overdose or a fall.

For Latino men and boys, the risk was up to 1.4 times higher than it was for whites. For Native American men, the risk was 1.2 to 1.7 times higher.

Overall, women's risk of being killed by police was roughly 20 times lower than the risk to men. Even so, there were clear differences by ethnicity and race.

For instance, black women were about 1.4 times as likely to be killed by police as white women, the researchers found. Native American women were from 1.1 to 2.1 times as likely to be killed as their white peers.

Among Asians and Pacific Islanders, both men and women were less than half as likely as their white peers to be killed by police.

And Latina women were 12% to 23% less likely than white women to meet that fate. (Edwards called that finding "interesting," but he hesitated to speculate about it without studying the issue further.)

Across all groups, younger adults were most at risk; the chances of being killed by police peaked between the ages of 20 and 35.

The early 20s are a particularly dangerous time for young men, the researchers found. During the study period, police use of force accounted for 1.6% of all deaths of black men between the ages of 20 and 24. It was also responsible for 1.2% of deaths of Latino and Native American men. However, police violence accounted for just 0.5% of deaths of white and Asian American men in that age range.

"We believe these numbers, if anything, are a little bit conservative, maybe a bit too low," Edwards said. "But we think that these are the best that can be done in terms of just getting a baseline risk estimate out there."

Justin Feldman, a social epidemiologist at the New York University School of Medicine, said the most striking result for him was the mortality risk for black men and boys, which he called "pretty staggering."

"That's quite meaningful," said Feldman, who was not involved in the study. "If it's not you being killed by police, it's someone you know or someone in your community."

Abigail Sewell, a sociologist at Emory University who did not work on the report, said she wasn't surprised by most of the study's results. But that did not change the gravity of the findings.

"Honestly, it was a really unsettling paper," she said.

Part of the solution may be to reduce unnecessary police contact in the first place, Sewell said. For example, programs that helped young men of color find jobs might help keep them off the streets and away from cops. Perhaps mental health professionals could be called upon to address psychiatric issues instead of asking police to do so, since they typically do not have training for such tasks.

If unnecessary police contact were eliminated, she said, the incidence of fatal police violence might be lower—and racial disparities might be diminished too.

"But I'm not sure if the disparities would disappear altogether," she said. "These women and these men ... are living in neighborhoods that are overpoliced, where the police are very brutal in the way they treat citizens."

Retired Police Maj. Neill Franklin also highlighted the need for cultural and logistical shifts in policing. He pointed to the "war on drugs" waged by the federal government as an example.

That campaign "is clearly a public health issue when it comes to addiction, but for decades we have been using our police departments as the tip of the spear in dealing with this public health issue," said Franklin, who now serves as executive director of the Law Enforcement Action Partnership, an advocacy group comprising criminal justice professionals.

That spear, he said, has often been pointed toward black communities in inner cities.

The study authors said other factors may also be at play. It's possible that the lightness or darkness of a person's skin tone within his or her racial and ethnic group could affect his or her risk. So could geography, if Latino citizens are treated differently in different states.

But in order to probe such questions, scientists say they need far more data than is currently available. Information on police stops, whether or not they result in an arrest, would be crucial in determining the extent to which racial bias plays a role in police contact.

Franklin, who spent much of his 34-year career in law enforcement in the Baltimore city and Maryland state police departments, agreed.

"We need to do a much better job on monitoring the interactions of our police officers as they're going about their daily duties," he said. "I think we would be foolish to believe that we have solved to any great extent the issue of racial profiling in this country regarding police."

Getting that data will require more cooperation from police departments across the country, the researchers added.

"The United States is unique among wealthy democracies in terms of the number of people that are killed by its police forces," Feldman said. "I think the No. 1 thing it comes down to is a lack of accountability by police departments, both legally and politically."

> *"Overall in 2015, black people were killed at twice the rate of white, Hispanic and native Americans. About 25% of the African Americans killed were unarmed, compared with 17% of white people."*

Young Black Men Have Bullseyes on Their Backs

Jon Swaine, Oliver Laughland, Jamiles Lartey, and Ciara McCarthy

In the following viewpoint, Jon Swaine, Oliver Laughland, Jamiles Lartey, and Ciara McCarthy report on the astonishingly disproportionate number of police-involved deaths of young Black males in the United States. The authors cite data that breaks down these deaths, showing a variety of root causes and how many of these deaths can be considered "justified." Shockingly, the federal government has not historically kept records of people killed by police, so such data—as well as public awareness of the issue—is relatively new. The authors are US-based reporters for the Guardian.

As you read, consider the following questions:

1. What progress do the authors report regarding police violence against African Americans?
2. Do you feel there is far greater awareness about treatment of Blacks by police since this viewpoint was first published in 2015?
3. How have mental issues contributed to fatal outcomes of confrontations between police and the public?

Young black men were nine times more likely than other Americans to be killed by police officers in 2015, according to the findings of a *Guardian* study that recorded a final tally of 1,134 deaths at the hands of law enforcement officers this year.

Despite making up only 2% of the total US population, African American males between the ages of 15 and 34 comprised more than 15% of all deaths logged this year by an ongoing investigation into the use of deadly force by police. Their rate of police-involved deaths was five times higher than for white men of the same age.

Paired with official government mortality data, this new finding indicates that about one in every 65 deaths of a young African American man in the US is a killing by police.

"This epidemic is disproportionately affecting black people," said Brittany Packnett, an activist and member of the White House taskforce on policing. "We are wasting so many promising young lives by continuing to allow this to happen."

Speaking in the same week that a police officer in Cleveland, Ohio, was cleared by a grand jury over the fatal shooting of Tamir Rice, a 12-year-old African American boy who was carrying a toy gun, Packnett said the criminal justice system was presenting "no deterrent" to the excessive use of deadly force by police. "Tamir didn't even live to be 15," she said.

Protests accusing law enforcement officers of being too quick to use lethal force against unarmed African Americans have spread across the country in the 16 months since dramatic unrest gripped

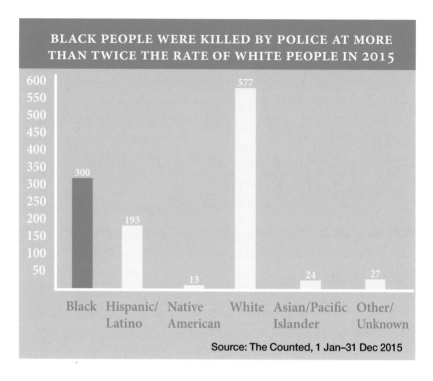

BLACK PEOPLE WERE KILLED BY POLICE AT MORE
THAN TWICE THE RATE OF WHITE PEOPLE IN 2015

Source: The Counted, 1 Jan–31 Dec 2015

Ferguson, Missouri, following the fatal police shooting of 18-year-old Michael Brown by a white officer.

Overall in 2015, black people were killed at twice the rate of white, Hispanic and native Americans. About 25% of the African Americans killed were unarmed, compared with 17% of white people. This disparity has narrowed since the database was first published on 1 June, at which point black people killed were found to be twice as likely to not have a weapon.

The *Guardian's* investigation, titled The Counted, began in response to widespread concern about the federal government's failure to keep any comprehensive record of people killed by police. Officials at the US Department of Justice have since begun testing a database that attempts to do so, directly drawing on The Counted's data and methodology.

The FBI also announced plans to overhaul its own count of homicides by police, which has been discredited by its reliance on the voluntary submission of data from a fraction of the country's

18,000 police departments. The *Guardian*'s total for 2015 was more than two and a half times greater than the 444 "justifiable homicides" logged by the FBI last year.

The FBI director, James Comey, said in October it was "embarrassing and ridiculous" that the government did not hold comprehensive statistics, and that it was "unacceptable" the *Guardian* and the *Washington Post*, which began publishing a database of fatal police shootings on 1 July, held better records. The Counted will continue into 2016.

Data collected by the *Guardian* this year highlighted the wide range of situations encountered by police officers across the US. Of the 1,134 people killed, about one in five were unarmed but another one in five fired shots of their own at officers before being killed. At least six innocent bystanders were killed by officers during violent incidents; eight police officers were killed by people who subsequently died and appeared in the database.

More than 21% of deadly incidents began with a complaint to police alleging domestic violence or some other domestic disturbance. About 16% arose from officers attempting to arrest a wanted person, execute a warrant or apprehend a fugitive. Another 14% of killings followed an attempted traffic or street stop, 13% came after someone committed a violent crime and 7% after a non-violent crime.

In addition to those killed after opening fire, 160 people were accused of refusing commands to drop a weapon. Another 157 were said to have pointed or levelled a gun or non-lethal gun at officers. Police alleged that 158 people killed had "charged," advanced at or fought with officers. And while 79 people were killed after allegedly "reaching for their waistband" or grabbing for a weapon, 44 attacked officers, some with knives and blades.

"It would appear that police officers are often confronting people who are armed, non-compliant and threatening," said David Klinger, an associate professor of criminology at the University of Missouri-St. Louis.

The extensive demographic detail gathered as part of the study also shed light on the diverse set of people who died during confrontations with law enforcement. The group ranged in age from six-year-old Jeremy Mardis, in Marksville, Louisiana, to 87-year-old Louis Becker in Catskill, New York. Officers killed 43 people who were 18 years old and younger.

Mental health crises contributed directly to dozens of police-involved deaths. In at least 92 cases that led to fatalities this year, police had been alerted over a suicidal person or someone who was harming him- or herself. In 28 other deadly incidents, relatives or associates later said that the person killed had been suicidal before they died.

RACIAL BIAS IN POLICE TRAFFIC STOPS

People of color living in the United States won't be surprised by the results of a recent study published by researchers from Stanford University. The Stanford Open Policing Project has "collected and standardized over 200 million records of traffic stop and search data from across the country," which resulted in sweeping evidence of "significant racial disparities in policing," according to a new report.

NBC News reviewed data from the project and noted that officers stop and search Black and Latinx drivers based on less evidence than what they require to stop and search White drivers. Meanwhile, White drivers "are more likely to be found with illegal items." From the report:

After accounting for age, gender and location, we find that officers ticket, search and arrest Black and Hispanic drivers more often than Whites. For example, when pulled over for speeding, Black drivers are 20 percent more likely to get a ticket (rather than a warning) than White drivers, and Hispanic drivers are 30 percent more likely to be ticketed than White drivers. Black and Hispanic motorists are about twice as likely to be searched compared to White drivers.

Of 29 military veterans who were killed by police in 2015, at least eight were said to have been suffering from post-traumatic stress disorder (PTSD) following their service. In all, mental health issues were reported in relation to 246 people killed by police this year—more than one in every five cases. On at least eight occasions, the death was officially ruled a suicide, prompting claims from relatives that officers were escaping scrutiny.

"We have a tremendous problem," said Dr. Daniel Reidenberg, the managing director of the National Council for Suicide Prevention. "In a society where firearms are as prevalent as they are, and where people know law enforcement are trained to respond to a certain situation in a certain way, we have a problem."

This study doesn't attempt to answer if the officers were knowingly policing with racial bias, but instead digs into the traffic stop data to "infer that race is a factor when people are pulled over—and that it's occuring across the country," NBC reports.
The Stanford Open Policing Project explains,

These patterns illustrate the disparate impact of policing on minority communities. However, as with stop rates, these disparities may not be due to bias. In nearly every jurisdiction, stopped Black and Hispanic drivers are searched more often than Whites. But if minorities also happen to carry contraband at higher rates, these higher search rates may stem from appropriate police work. Disentangling discrimination from effective policing is challenging and requires more subtle statistical analysis.

Sharad Goel, an assistant professor in management science and engineering at Stanford and a co-author of the study, spoke to NBC about the group's findings. "Because of this analysis," Goel began, "we're able to get to that anecdotal story to say this is really happening."
The team's research relied on stats from state and city agencies, however not all police agencies keep track of this information or are willing to share it.

"New Report Analyzes Racial Bias in Police Traffic Stops," by Shani Saxon, Race Forward, March 14, 2019.

Regional disparities also emerged from the year's data. Earlier this month, the *Guardian* published a series of special reports on Kern County, California, where police killed more people relative to the size of its population than anywhere else in the country. Law enforcement officers there killed more people in 2015 than the NYPD, which has 23 times as many officers policing a population 10 times as big.

Following a spate of killings in recent weeks, New Mexico's 21 deaths in 2015 represented the highest per-capita rate of any state. New Mexico's rate of one killing by police for every 99,300 residents was more than 10 times greater than that of Rhode Island, where only one person among a population of more than a million was killed by law enforcement.

The death of Kenneth Stephens, 56, in Burlington, Vermont, last week meant that all 50 states and the District of Columbia had at least one death caused by police in 2015.

Only one of the 21 people killed by police in New Mexico, however, was unarmed. By contrast nine of the 25 people killed in New York state were unarmed, and seven of these were black men. While five of Georgia's 38 deaths followed a suspect being shocked with a Taser—the highest proportion in the country—no Taser-involved deaths were recorded in more than half a dozen states.

In all, 89% of deaths by police in 2015 were caused by gunshot, 4% were Taser-related, 4% were deaths in custody following physical confrontations and 3% were deaths of people struck by police officers driving vehicles.

The Counted found that in at least 255 deaths in 2015, the actions of police officers involved had been ruled justified. These rulings were typically made by a district attorney who worked alongside the department of the officers involved in prosecuting everyday crimes. About a quarter of the justified cases were decided on by a grand jury of the public.

Law enforcement officers were charged with crimes in relation to 18 of 2015's deadly incidents—10 shootings, four deadly vehicle crashes and four deaths in custody.

By the end of the year, one officer had been acquitted of charges relating to a fatal shooting in Pennsylvania, and the first attempt at prosecuting one of the officers involved in the deadly arrest of Freddie Gray in Baltimore had ended in a mistrial. Two deputies in Georgia charged over the in-custody death of Matthew Ajibade were cleared of manslaughter but convicted of cruelty, perjury and falsifying paperwork.

Philip Stinson, an associate professor at Bowling Green University who monitors the subject, said the number of officers being charged had risen sharply this year. "There is more public awareness, and I do think that in the past few years the veracity of police officers is being questioned more, after their statements were shown to not be consistent with video evidence," he said.

> *"Rates of post-traumatic stress disorder among police officers are much higher than among the general population; around one in four police officers has suicidal thoughts."*

Don't Blame Police Racism for America's Violence Epidemic

Zaid Jilani

In the following viewpoint Zaid Jilani argues that gang violence and other issues in America's inner cities produce equally brutal responses by law enforcement. The author cites a disturbing statistic that homicide is the leading cause of death among African American teenagers, at a rate nearly twenty times higher than that of white teenagers. Although some of those youth had been unarmed when they were killed by police officers, the narrative that racism drove those killings is misleading. In fact, gang-related murders are a far more significant and widespread problem. Zaid Jilani is a journalist and fellow in political and social polarization at UC Berkeley's Greater Good Science Center.

As you read, consider the following questions:

1. Why is it important to understand this issue from the perspective of police officers?
2. Does Zaid Jilani argue that racism does not exist in American law enforcement?
3. How does the author use Black-on-Black homicide statistics to make his point?

In political debates about incidents of police officers shooting and killing Americans, a consistent narrative has emerged: There is an epidemic of white police officers targeting unarmed African Americans—the reason being that America's police forces are so racially biased that they value the lives of blacks less than they value the lives of whites. Given the horrifying history of racism in the United States, this was never a far-fetched thesis. This phenomenon is at the heart of Black Lives Matter, a movement that has pushed media and politicians to consider the issue of police abuse as a matter of racial injustice.

"Black men, unarmed, black teenagers, unarmed, and black children, unarmed, are being killed at a frightening level right now, including by members of law enforcement without accountability and without justice," then-Texas Democratic congressman and now presidential candidate Beto O'Rourke told an audience last year. O'Rourke made the statement as part of a larger speech in support of NFL players such as Colin Kaepernick, who took a knee during the national anthem to protest racism and police brutality.

The definition of "frightening" is subjective, but as the *Washington Post* noted later, three unarmed black teenagers aged 18 and under were shot and killed by police between 2015 and 2018. During the same time period, "six teenagers and three children who were white or Hispanic—and unarmed—were fatally shot [by police]."

If you zoom out and look at killings of African American minors outside the context of police actions, the picture is actually far more grim. "Homicide is the leading cause of death for non-Hispanic black male teenagers," notes the Centers for Disease Control, while accidents remain the top cause of death for teens from other racial backgrounds. The homicide rate in 2017 for black teens was almost 16 times higher than the rate among white teens.

Putting statistics aside, is it true that police killings of African Americans are driven by racial bias—by white police officers with a Jim-Crow mindset who view blacks as less than human? A new study by a group of American researchers offers some insight, and suggests that the conventional narrative is misleading.

Lead researcher David Johnson, psychologist and postdoctoral fellow at the University of Maryland, led a team that analyzed police shootings in America by building a database of 917 fatal officer-involved shootings (FOIS) from over 650 different police departments in 2015. They looked at both the race of the police officers doing the shooting and the races of the individuals killed. If America had an epidemic of white-on-black police shootings, you would expect that white police officers would be more likely to shoot African Americans. But that isn't what they found.

Instead, they found that when the data is sorted according to the race of the involved officers, "as the percentage of black officers who shot in a FOIS increased, a person fatally shot was more likely to be black…than white. As the percentage of Hispanic officers who shot in a FOIS increased, a person fatally shot was more likely to be Hispanic…than white." It is actually more likely for black and Hispanic citizens to be killed by black and Hispanic police officers than by white officers.

This doesn't mean that the black and Hispanic officers are more biased against fellow black and Hispanic residents. Instead, the researchers postulate that this may be due to "simple overlap between officer and county demographics." Police departments in areas with greater numbers of ethnic minorities tend to have a more diverse police force. Indeed, the paper notes that "when county variables were included, the relationship between officer and civilian race was attenuated or eliminated….This suggests that the association between officer race and black and Hispanic disparities in FOIS largely occur because officers and civilians are drawn from the same population."

In an interview, Johnson stressed that we shouldn't conclude that just because racial diversity in a police force does not reduce lethal shootings doesn't mean it has no value. "Another possibility is we might find that officer race matters more for other kinds of force, so baton use, taser use, those sorts of things," he said. "Our data is just about shootings that resulted in fatality….What I want to be clear on, is we don't find evidence for racial disparities, at least as tied to officer race. It's not the case that white officers seem to be primarily responsible for these shootings. But we're not at all trying to argue that the police are, say, free of racial bias. The data we have just don't answer that kind of question."

This isn't the only research that shows that white officers aren't more likely to shoot black citizens. Last year, a study from Rutgers University found that "white officers are no more likely to use lethal force against minorities than nonwhite officers," in the words of lead researcher Charles Menifield.

But what of the disproportionate number of black citizens killed by police every year? As a Vox writer has noted, in 2012, 31 percent of all people killed by police were African American, while only about 13 percent of the total American population is black. Isn't that a sign of racial bias?

The new study disputes the use of this metric as a means to prove bias. "Using population as a benchmark makes the strong assumption that white and black civilians have equal exposure to situations that result in FOIS," it writes. "If there are racial differences in exposure to these situations, calculations of racial disparity based on population benchmarks will be misleading."

The researchers found that the factor that most predicted the race of a citizen fatally shot was homicide rates for those groups in particular counties. For instance, in counties where whites committed a higher percentage of homicides, victims of police shootings are 3.5 times more likely to be white; in counties where blacks commit more homicides, victims are 3.7 times more likely to be black.

This suggests that violent crime rates correlate to—and perhaps may be used to predict—fatal interactions between police and citizens. The *Washington Post*'s police shootings database, which serves to document every fatal police shooting in the country, provides more evidence in this regard. Of the 505 fatal police shootings cataloged in 2019 as of this writing, only 20 involved a victim who was unarmed (although 12 of the victims carried toy weapons). If these victims were being targeted for reasons unrelated to their possible identity as criminal suspects, one would not expect that 96 percent would be armed.

This isn't to say that all police shootings are justified or unavoidable. The state should never take any life if it has any alternative to neutralizing someone who poses a threat. (I oppose capital punishment under the same principle.) But it does suggest that police are using violence largely because they find themselves in dangerous situations, not because they are acting on racial animus.

The percentage of African Americans killed every year by police is tied to the homicide rate among African Americans. I am certainly not endorsing irrational and unscientific theories about some kind of "inherent" violent attitude among African Americans: The majority of African-Americans never commit any violent crime whatsoever, and homicides in the United States are highly concentrated among a few communities with high poverty, high levels of segregation, and inadequate policing (all of which are, of course, indirectly or even directly related to the country's history of racism). Some prosperous African American communities, like Prince George's County in Maryland, are relatively safe and see little of both common homicide and police brutality compared to, say, West Baltimore. And we shouldn't forget that around half of the people killed every year by police are white, and that Johnson's study found the same relationship between homicide rates and police shootings for whites as it did for blacks.

But we should recognize that policies such as increasing the racial diversity of our police forces won't accomplish very much if non-white police officers are just as likely to use deadly force. Implicit bias training won't stop police shootings if they are mostly occurring in dangerous situations in which the victim is armed and connected to some form of crime. Instead, a race-neutral approach may be the best way to lower the number of victims of police shootings.

Some parts of this approach are by now well-known. More and more police departments are being taught to de-escalate tense situations, so police can verbally calm down violent criminals as an alternative to using force.

But so long as parts of America have so much violent crime, police will inevitably respond with lethal force. We can't keep writing articles noting that Norway's police are far less lethal than America's without noting that America has more guns than people and that there were a total of 25 murders in Norway in all of 2017. The city of Chicago, which has around half the population of Norway, on the other hand, lost 650 people to homicide the same year. It stands to reason that Norway's police simply don't have to deal with the same social problems and extreme rates of violence that Chicago's do, so of course they'll be using less force, and using it less often.

Progressives are quick to (correctly) note that the roots of crime are socially and culturally constructed. But they are more reluctant to accept the reality that one reason for the prevalence of police brutality may be that police are operating in brutal environments. Rates of post-traumatic stress disorder among police officers are much higher than among the general population; around one in four police officers has suicidal thoughts.

In the *New Yorker* profile of Darren Wilson—the police officer who killed the African American teenager Michael Brown in the city of Ferguson, Missouri, in 2014, setting off the Black Lives Matter movement—what struck me the most was how much violence Wilson had encountered before he ever met Brown. At one stop, he was met with the bodies of two dead women and a two-year-old child covered in blood crawling between them. It is possible that the anti-social or violent behavior by both common criminals and the police is influenced by the environments they live and work in as well.

In other words: If we want to reduce police shootings, we have to reduce violent crime. "The strongest implication from our data is if we can reduce those crime rates, we are going to decrease the number of people who are fatally shot by police," Johnson said.

There is no silver bullet for how to do so, but we do know of strategies that have worked in the past—ranging from reducing lead exposure, to reducing economic inequality, to increasing police levels (and training), to community activism and interventions based on changing the norms around violence in an area.

A recent study published in the journal *Demography* found that 17 percent of the reduction in the life expectancy gap between white and black men could be attributed to the reduction in homicides that occurred in the 1990s and early 2000s. For all of their righteous criticism of politicians such as Bill Clinton and Joe Biden—the architects of the '90s crime-reduction policy in the United States— Black Lives Matter activists are unlikely to admit that reducing violent crime has saved, and would continue to save, orders of magnitude more black lives than any number of police-focused reforms (and the lives of countless others).

Four years ago, the national media and liberal activists converged on the city of Baltimore, Maryland, following the shocking and unconscionable death of Freddie Gray, a man who died in police custody in 2015. Intense protests and riots occurred in the aftermath, and the city engaged in a consent decree with the Department of Justice to reform itself. The government's investigations did indeed find corrupt and unconstitutional practices by some of the city's police force.

But as Baltimore engaged in much-needed reforms to prevent police brutality and heal relations with the citizenry, it also effectively de-policed much of the city. There were 39,654 arrests in Baltimore in 2014, compared to 25,820 arrests in 2016, while homicides increased from 211 to 318 in that period. By November 2017, gun arrests were down 67 percent from the previous year.

Reverend Kinji Scott, a community activist in the city, told me last year that he blames this de-policing for the spike in homicides. "We saw the police department arrest less during a period of high crime," he said. "So what happened is you have a community of emboldened criminals." The issue is personal for Scott: He lost a cousin to murder in Chicago, and his brother was murdered in St. Louis. In all three cities, the homicide clearance rate—the proportion of cases in which police are able to charge someone for a crime—is abysmal. Baltimore's clearance rate in 2018 was 43 percent; Chicago's police are solving fewer than 1 in 6 murders. It would be nice to see liberal activists expressing as much concern about these legions of lost lives as those few taken by police.

According to the *Washington Post*'s police-shooting database, 223 African Americans were killed in police-involved shootings in 2017. Each of those deaths is a tragedy, even if police had no choice in many or most of these instances. Every one of us carries a precious soul from the moment of our birth to the instant of our death, and we should prioritize saving lives to such an extent that we shouldn't rest until the number is zero—for African Americans and everyone else. But that same year, we saw 7,851 black victims of homicide, according to the FBI's Uniform Crime Report. That's a 35-to-1 ratio of killings between the two tallies. Does it make sense that our outrage be guided by the identity of the shooter—whether it's the color of his skin, or the presence of a police uniform?

There's some good news out there, too. The New York Police Department shot 341 people in 1971 and just 19 in 2017. The city is much safer than it was then. In 1972, there were 1,691 murders in the city while in 2018 there were only 289. More sophisticated training and technology probably explain some of the decline in police shootings, but a much less violent ecosystem overall probably explains the rest. That should be the goal for the whole country—even if the dream of turning the United States into a place that's as peaceful as Norway might never be realized.

> "The anti-profiling crusaders have
> created a headlong movement
> without defining their central term
> and without providing a shred
> of credible evidence that 'racial
> profiling' is a widespread police
> practice."

Racial Profiling Is a Myth

Heather Mac Donald

*In the following excerpted viewpoint, Heather Mac Donald argues
that racial profiling is little more than myth. It is important to note
that this viewpoint was originally written in 2001, as mainstream
leaders began to call an end to racial profiling and other racist
policies. Heather Mac Donald writes for the Manhattan Institute
for Policy Research, a conservative think tank whose stated mission
is to develop and disseminate new ideas that foster greater economic
choice and individual responsibility.*

"The Myth of Racial Profiling," by Heather Mac Donald, Manhattan Institute for Policy
Research, Inc., 2001. Reprinted with permission from the Manhattan Institute's *City
Journal*.

As you read, consider the following questions:

1. What question does the author pose to former president George W. Bush?
2. What has changed in terms of policing since this viewpoint was first published?
3. How does the author use specific incidents on the roads to make compelling arguments in her favor?

The anti-"racial profiling" juggernaut must be stopped, before it obliterates the crime-fighting gains of the last decade, especially in inner cities. The anti-profiling crusade thrives on an ignorance of policing and a willful blindness to the demographics of crime. Yet politicians are swarming on board. In February, President George W. Bush joined the rush, declaring portentously: "Racial profiling is wrong, and we will end it in America."

Too bad no one asked President Bush: "What exactly do you mean by 'racial profiling,' and what evidence do you have that it exists?" For the anti-profiling crusaders have created a headlong movement without defining their central term and without providing a shred of credible evidence that "racial profiling" is a widespread police practice.

The ultimate question in the profiling controversy is whether the disproportionate involvement of blacks and Hispanics with law enforcement reflects police racism or the consequences of disproportionate minority crime. Anti-profiling activists hope to make police racism an all but irrebuttable presumption whenever enforcement statistics show high rates of minority stops and arrests. But not so fast.

Two meanings of "racial profiling" intermingle in the activists' rhetoric. What we may call "hard" profiling uses race as the only factor in assessing criminal suspiciousness: an officer sees a black person and, without more to go on, pulls him over for a pat-down on the chance that he may be carrying drugs or weapons. "Soft" racial profiling is using race as one factor among others in gauging criminal suspiciousness: the highway police, for example, have intelligence that Jamaican drug posses with a fondness for Nissan Pathfinders are transporting marijuana along the northeast corridor. A New Jersey trooper sees a black motorist speeding in a Pathfinder and pulls him over in the hope of finding drugs.

The racial profiling debate focuses primarily on highway stops. The police are pulling over a disproportionate number of minority drivers for traffic offenses, goes the argument, in order to look for drugs. Sure, the driver committed an infraction, but the reason the trooper chose to stop him, rather than the speeder next to him, was his race.

But the profiling critics also fault both the searches that sometimes follow a highway stop and the tactics of urban policing. Any evaluation of the evidence for, and the appropriateness of, the use of race in policing must keep these contexts distinct. Highway stops should almost always be color-blind, I'll argue, but in other policing environments (including highway searches), where an officer has many clues to go on, race may be among them. Ironically, effective urban policing shows that the more additional factors an officer has in his criminal profile, the more valid race becomes— and the less significant, almost to the point of irrelevance.

Before reviewing the evidence that profiling critics offer, recall the demands that the police face every day, far from anti-police agitators and their journalist acolytes.

February 22, 2001, a town-hall meeting at P.S. 153 in Harlem between New York mayor Rudolph Giuliani and Harlem residents: a woman sarcastically asks Giuliani if police officers downtown are paid more than uptown officers, "because we don't have any quality of life in Harlem, none whatsoever. Drug dealers are allowed to stand out in front of our houses every day, to practically invade us, and nothing's done about it." Another woman complains that dealers are back on the street the day after being arrested, and notes that "addicts are so bold that we have to get off the sidewalk and go around them!" She calls for the declaration of a state of emergency. A man wonders if cop-basher congressman Charles

Rangel, present at the meeting, could "endow the police with more power," and suggests that the NYPD coordinate with the federal Drug Enforcement Administration, the INS, and the IRS to bring order to the streets.

The audience meets Giuliani's assertions that the police have brought crime down sharply in Harlem with hoots of derision. No one mentions "police brutality."

Valentine's Day, 2001, a police-community meeting at Harlem's 28th Precinct: an elegant man in an angora turtleneck, tiny blue glasses, and a shadow of a goatee breaks a local taboo by asking what the precinct is doing "to address dealing on the corners." Most residents shrink from mentioning the problem at precinct meetings for fear of retaliation from dealers. A tense silence falls. The man, a restaurant investor, tells me, "If this was 59th and Park, the police wouldn't allow these individuals to hang out on the corner." He can't understand why there's no "immediate result," if the police have in fact been cracking down on drug-dealing. "I don't think it should be so hard to dismantle," he says impatiently.

February 12, 2001, the fifth floor of a hulking yellow apartment building on Lenox Road in Flatbush, Brooklyn: two officers from the 67th Precinct investigate an anonymous call reporting a group of youths smoking marijuana in the hallway. The boys have disappeared. As officers check the stairwell, a gaunt middle-aged man sporting a wildly patterned black-and-white tie courteously introduces himself as Mr. Johnson, the building superintendent. After slowly bending down to pick up a discarded cigarette butt, he asks politely if anything more can be done about the kids who come from the next building to smoke pot in his hallway.

This is the demand—often angry, sometimes wistful—that urban police forces constantly hear: get rid of the drugs! These recent appeals come after the most successful war on crime that New York City has ever conducted. A decade and a half ago, when drug-related drive-by shootings became epidemic, inner-city residents nationwide were calling even more frantically for protection from drug violence. When New Jersey, a key state on the drug corridor from Central America to New England, sent its state highway troopers to do foot patrols in Camden and Trenton, residents met them with cheers.

In New York, the mayhem eventually led to the development of the Giuliani administration's assertive policing that strives, quite successfully, to prevent crime from happening. Outside of New York, the widespread pleas to stop drug violence led the Drug Enforcement Administration to enlist state highway police in their anti-drug efforts. The DEA and the Customs Service had been using intelligence about drug routes and the typical itineraries of couriers to interdict drugs at airports; now the interdiction war would expand to the nation's highways, the major artery of the cocaine trade.

ZERO TOLERANCE

Zero tolerance.

When it comes to community crime fighting, those two words are music to the ears of residents and business owners who want to live and work in safe neighborhoods.

While it is the ultimate goal of law enforcement, absolute zero tolerance is realistically unattainable when so many commit crimes and there are too few officers.

Still, in Niagara Falls, the police department last week undertook what officials say will be a series of saturation patrols aimed at cracking down on wrongdoers in areas where statistics show criminal activity is most prevalent.

Members of the department's Roving Anti-Crime unit, also known as RAC, targeted Highland and Whitney avenues and 17th and 18th streets as part of their new approach to attacking gangs and violent crimes. The so-called "focused deterrence" concept is one of several aspects of the Gun Involved Violence Elimination, or GIVE, an anti-crime initiative funded by the New York State Department of Criminal Justice Services.

Elements of the program were introduced to Falls officers and brass about a year ago by representatives from the Justice Department and will help the Falls department better focus on

The DEA taught state troopers some common identifying signs of drug couriers: nervousness; conflicting information about origin and destination cities among vehicle occupants; no luggage for a long trip; lots of cash; lack of a driver's license or insurance; the spare tire in the back seat; rental license plates or plates from key source states like Arizona and New Mexico; loose screws or scratches near a vehicle's hollow spaces, which can be converted to hiding places for drugs and guns. The agency also shared intelligence about the types of cars that couriers favored on certain routes, as well as about the ethnic makeup of drug-trafficking organizations. A typical DEA report from the early 1990s noted that "large-scale interstate trafficking networks controlled by Jamaicans, Haitians, and black street gangs dominate the manufacture and distribution

"chronic offenders," familiar suspects who are deemed worthy of extra attention, enforcement and prosecution.

During last week's exercise, Falls officers joined deputies from the Niagara County Sheriff's Office, the Lewiston Police Department and county probation and state parole officers to target members of a group known as 1800 or 18 Block, a local gang with several members who are no strangers to law enforcements.

By the end of the two-day law enforcement blitz, 37 arrests had been made. Police say the amount is about three times the average for a typical weekend. Ten of those arrests involved narcotics offenses and five of them occurred as part of a single traffic stop on Eighth Street. The officers had 74 "stops" or encounters with individuals, including a number of members of the 18 Block gang. Nine of the people who were arrested were brought in on outstanding warrants.

"We are sending a message that we are going to be around with a police presence," said Administrative Capt. Michael Trane. "We know that the activity of these individuals is driving crime and violence in some neighborhoods and it has to stop. Until it stops, we are going to stop them and if there's a reason to, we will arrest them. They need to change."

"EDITORIAL: Police Presence in High-Crime Areas Welcomed," *Niagara Gazette*, May 11, 2016.

of crack." The 1999 "Heroin Trends" report out of Newark declared that "predominant wholesale traffickers are Colombian, followed by Dominicans, Chinese, West African/Nigerian, Pakistani, Hispanic and Indian. Mid-levels are dominated by Dominicans, Colombians, Puerto Ricans, African-Americans and Nigerians."

According to the racial profiling crowd, the war on drugs immediately became a war on minorities, on the highways and off. Their alleged evidence for racial profiling comes in two varieties: anecdotal, which is of limited value, and statistical, which on examination proves entirely worthless.

The most notorious racial profiling anecdote may have nothing to do with racial profiling at all. On April 23, 1998, two New Jersey state troopers pulled over a van that they say was traveling at 74 miles an hour in a 55-mile-an-hour zone on the New Jersey Turnpike. As they approached on foot, the van backed toward them, knocking one trooper down, hitting the patrol car, and then getting sideswiped as it entered the traffic lane still in reverse. The troopers fired 11 rounds at the van, wounding three of the four passengers, two critically.

Attorneys for the van passengers deny that the van was speeding. The only reason the cops pulled it over, critics say, was that its occupants were black and Hispanic.

If the troopers' version of the incident proves true, it is hard to see how racial profiling enters the picture. The van's alleged speed would have legitimately drawn the attention of the police. As for the shooting: whether justified or not, it surely was prompted by the possibly deadly trajectory of the van, not the race of the occupants. Nevertheless, on talk show after talk show, in every newspaper story denouncing racial profiling, the turnpike shooting has come to symbolize the lethal dangers of "driving while black."

Less notoriously, black motorists today almost routinely claim that the only reason they are pulled over for highway stops is their race. Once they are pulled over, they say, they are subject to harassment, including traumatic searches. Some of these tales are undoubtedly true. Without question, there are obnoxious officers out there, and some officers may ignore their training and target minorities. But since the advent of video cameras in patrol cars, installed in the wake of the racial profiling controversy, most charges of police racism, testified to under oath, have been disproved as lies.

The allegation that police systematically single out minorities for unjustified law enforcement ultimately stands or falls on numbers. In suits against police departments across the country, the ACLU and the Justice Department have waved studies aplenty allegedly demonstrating selective enforcement. None of them holds up to scrutiny.

The typical study purports to show that minority motorists are subject to disproportionate traffic stops. Trouble is, no one yet has devised an adequate benchmark against which to measure if police are pulling over, searching, or arresting "too many" blacks and Hispanics. The question must always be: too many compared with what? Even anti-profiling activists generally concede that police pull drivers over for an actual traffic violation, not for no reason whatsoever, so a valid benchmark for stops would be the number of serious traffic violators, not just drivers. If it turns out that minorities tend to drive more recklessly, say, or have more equipment violations, you'd expect them to be subject to more stops. But to benchmark accurately, you'd also need to know the number of miles driven by different racial groups, so that you'd compare stops per man-mile, not just per person. Throw in age demographics as well: if a minority group has more young people—read: immature drivers—than whites do, expect more traffic stops of that group. The final analysis must then compare police deployment patterns with racial driving patterns: if more police are on the road when a higher proportion of blacks are driving—on weekend nights, say—stops of blacks will rise.

No traffic-stop study to date comes near the requisite sophistication. Most simply compare the number of minority stops with some crude population measure, and all contain huge and fatal data gaps. An ACLU analysis of Philadelphia traffic stops, for example, merely used the percentage of blacks in the 1990 census as a benchmark for stops made seven years later. In about half the stops that the ACLU studied, the officer did not record the race of the motorist. The study ignored the rate of traffic violations by race, so its grand conclusion of selective enforcement is meaningless.

> *"When the police search black, Latino and Native American people, they are less likely to find drugs, weapons or other contraband compared to when they search white people."*

Black People in California Are Stopped Far More Often by the Police

Darwin BondGraham

In the following viewpoint, Darwin BondGraham uses both statistical data and the experiences of interviewed individuals who were pulled over and confronted by police while behind the wheel, particularly in the state of California. The author argues that African Americans are pulled over and questioned at a far greater rate than white drivers in terms of percentage of population. However, the issue is more nuanced than the numbers provided by data. Darwin BondGraham is a reporter on the Guardian's *Guns and Lies in America project.*

As you read, consider the following questions:

1. How can greater transparency among police departments lead to positive change regarding the issue of "driving while Black"?
2. How does the viewpoint dispute the argument that people of color are stopped more often by police for legitimate reasons?
3. Would more hiring of Black officers aid in the fight against racial profiling on America's roads?

Black people in California were stopped by police officers much more frequently than other racial groups in 2018, and police were more likely to use force against them, new statistics from eight large law enforcement agencies in the state reveal.

Twenty eight per cent of all persons stopped by Los Angeles police officers during the last six months of 2018 were black, while black people account for just 9% of the city's population, the data shows. In San Francisco, the black population has shrunk over several decades to just 5% of the city's total population, but 26% of all stops carried out by the SFPD from July through December of 2018 were of black people—marking the widest racial disparity in police stops of the eight reporting agencies.

According to the new data, black people are much more likely to have firearms pointed at them by police officers. They also are more likely to be detained, handcuffed and searched. At the same time, when the police search black, Latino and Native American people, they are less likely to find drugs, weapons or other contraband compared to when they search white people.

The stark findings are based on an analysis of records of 1.8 million people stopped by the eight largest police agencies in California in 2018. The data was collected by each police agency and provided to the California Department of Justice under a 2015 state law that mandates efforts to eliminate racial profiling by law enforcement.

RACIAL DISPARITIES IN CALIFORNIA POLICE STOPS	
28%	Share of drivers stopped by LAPD who were black. Black people account for just 9% of LA's population.
26%	Share of drivers stopped by SFPD who were black. Black people account for just 5% of San Francisco's population.
19%	Share of drivers stopped by SDPD who were black. Only 6% of San Diego's population is black.

The racial disparities revealed in the new statistics reflect the findings of older studies about racial profiling in US police departments that were based on smaller, less-detailed data sets. But California's new numbers make up the largest-ever dataset compiled about police stops in the US, and they lend considerable support to minority groups who have long complained about biased policing.

In Los Angeles, "black people in particular, and Latinos, are fearful of the police and are constantly having their dignity compromised by unwarranted stops and searches," said Alberto Retana, the CEO of the Community Coalition of Los Angeles, one of the groups in a new coalition seeking to eliminate racial profiling called Push LA.

Los Angeles police are continuing to use aggressive tactics in black and Latino neighborhoods, Retana said, even though violent crime rates in the city have dropped to historic lows.

Bryant Mangum said he has been pulled over by the LAPD approximately 30 times over the past couple years. The father of three lives in South Central Los Angeles and works in a warehouse. He also runs a startup that helps elderly people take trash out of their houses to the curb, and he is on the board of a not-for-profit that helps parolees start their own businesses.

Still, Mangum, who is black, feels harassed by the police.

"At night it never fails, I don't get a ticket or explanation," said Mangum. "They pull me out of the car, I'm handcuffed, and they search my car, for I don't know what."

A Longstanding Problem

The 2018 police data included numbers from the Los Angeles, San Diego and San Francisco police departments, the Los Angeles sheriff's department, Riverside county sheriff's department, San Bernardino county sheriff's department, San Diego county sheriff's department and the California Highway Patrol.

Seven additional medium-sized California departments are currently collecting stop data and will submit it for analysis next year. By 2022, every police force and sheriff's office in the state will be gathering and reporting stop data, providing the first ever view of an entire state's police interactions with the public.

The findings for Los Angeles come after one particular police unit, Metropolitan Division, faced intense scrutiny over an *LA Times* investigation that showed that about half the people stopped by its officers were black. Although the data examined by the *Times* couldn't prove bias, the sheer scale of the disparity was enough to cause LAPD's chief to order the unit to draw back on random vehicle stops.

For the city of San Diego, the 2018 data showed that black people accounted for 19% of all stops by the San Diego police last year even though only 6% of the city's population is black. Black people were 25% more likely to be searched, 8% more likely to be arrested without a warrant and 59% more likely to have force used against them during a stop, according to an analysis by the advocacy organization Campaign Zero.

In San Francisco, SFPD now stops black people at rates over five times their representation in the city's overall population, according to the 2018 data.

The disparity is a significant increase since the 1990s, when activists in northern California urged the San Francisco police to reduce the disproportionate numbers of black and Latino people stopped by police in the city. In 2002, the ACLU of Northern California accused the San Francisco police of being "in denial" over racial profiling after a study showed that black people were pulled over by the SFPD "at rates over twice their representation in the population."

In 2016, following a scandal involving at least 14 SFPD officers who exchanged racist, homophobic and transphobic text messages, the San Francisco district attorney convened a Blue Ribbon Panel of experts to propose reforms. The panel's final report found that SFPD officers more frequently asked black and Latino people for permission to search them compared to whites, even though white people who were searched were more likely to have contraband on them.

Numerous individuals have accused the SFPD of racially biased policing, including a 2018 lawsuit brought by people arrested in a 2013-2014 narcotics sting operation. The plaintiffs in the case allege that SFPD officers targeted only black people and ignored drug sales conducted by people of other races.

SFPD did not immediately respond to a request for comment.

"A Remarkable Opportunity"

Law enforcement groups opposed the Racial and Identity Profiling Act of 2015, which mandated the collection of the stop data and established the Ripa Board. The California State Sheriffs' Association argued that collecting the data is burdensome for officers and detracts from their ability to fight crime. Between 1997 and 2006, five similar bills that would have mandated stop data collection or prescribed racial bias training for police officers were vetoed or killed in the legislature following police union lobbying.

But advocates and policymakers have heralded the collection and disclosure of the statistics, while academics, community groups and police are being encouraged to drill into the data to better understand disparities in policing.

"It's an ambitious and cutting-edge effort," said Andrea Guerrero, the executive director of the Alliance San Diego, a community organization. Guerrero serves on the Racial and Identity Profiling Advisory Board, which was created in 2015 by the state legislature to oversee California's stop data collection and analysis effort.

"We've long had concerns about racial profiling and bias in policing here in San Diego county," Guerrero said. "The data is helpful to us, as it is across the state, in validating those concerns."

"As in other parts of the state, black San Diegans are being stopped and searched at higher rates, even though recovery of contraband is at much lower rates compared to white San Diegans."

But how to use California's new stop data going forward remains a contentious issue.

At a 20 November meeting in Oakland, Ripa board members debated the different methodologies for analyzing the new data for the board's 2020 annual report.

The King county sheriff, David Robinson, and the Morgan Hill police chief, David Swing, advocated for employing a method that compares stops at night versus daytime. The "veil of darkness" often shows that black people are more likely to be stopped at night than white people, a possible indication that racially biased policing isn't influencing who is pulled over because officers are less likely to be able to see a person's race in the dark.

"I like the veil of darkness," Robinson said at the meeting. "It just gives us another piece of the puzzle."

Other board members argued against including the veil of darkness method in the Ripa board's report, saying the assumption that officers can't see a driver's race at night isn't accurate, and that there are other reasons stops of black people might increase at night.

Matthew Ross, a research assistant professor at New York University who studies police stop data in other states, said there is no one best method of analysis.

"The whole issue of racial profiling is nuanced and there's things the data can't tell you," Ross said. "But it can show you where to extend those resources for a deeper dive."

Ross credited the veil of darkness method for overcoming previous limits of other analyses, but he said it has its own flaws.

One possible reason police pull fewer black people over during the day is that black people are aware of their racial visibility in daylight, therefore they overcompensate and drive more carefully giving police fewer opportunities to stop them.

Another possible reason is that police resources are redeployed when the sun goes down, said Ross, concentrating officers in predominantly black and Latino neighborhoods.

In Connecticut, where a similar state board is gathering and analyzing stop data, Ross said one recent debate between police and community advocates about how stop data should be interpreted concerned stops of motorists that ended with only a warning given by an officer.

"If you have a higher rate of warnings for minority motorists, to the policing community it means they're giving people breaks," said Ross. "But to advocates, it means you're stopping minorities and looking for reasons to search them."

Advocates in California say they welcome the opportunity to discuss racial disparities in policing with the new data, complexity and all.

"I think the data presents a remarkable opportunity for police departments across the state to reduce their racist practices," said Retana, the CEO of the Community Coalition of Los Angeles.

"People usually use data against us," he added. "Now is the time to use it in the people's interests."

Periodical and Internet Sources Bibliography

The following articles have been selected to supplement the diverse views presented in this chapter.

American Civil Liberties Union, "What 100 Years of History Tells Us About Racism in Policing," December 11, 2020. https://www.aclu .org/news/criminal-law-reform/what-100-years-of-history-tells -us-about-racism-in-policing

Lydia Denworth, "A Civil Rights Expert Explains the Social Science of Police Racism," *Scientific American*, June 4, 2020. https://www .scientificamerican.com/article/a-civil-rights-expert-explains -the-social-science-of-police-racism

Drew Desilver, Michael Lipka, and Dalia Fahmy, "10 Things We Know About Race and Policing in the US," Pew Research Center, June 3, 2020. https://www.pewresearch.org/fact -tank/2020/06/03/10-things-we-know-about-race-and-policing -in-the-u-s

Clarence Edwards, "Race and the Police," National Police Foundation. https://www.policefoundation.org/race-and-the-police

Michael A. Fletcher, "For Black Motorists, a Never-Ending Fear of Being Stopped, *National Geographic*, April 2018. https://www .nationalgeographic.com/magazine/2018/04/the-stop-race -police-traffic/

David A. Harris, "Racial Profiling: Past, Present, and Future," American Bar Association. https://www.americanbar.org/groups /criminal_justice/publications/criminal-justice-magazine/2020 /winter/racial-profiling-past-present-and-future/

P. R. Lockhart, "Living While Black and the Criminalization of Blackness," Vox, August 1, 2018. https://www.vox.com /explainers/2018/8/1/17616528/racial-profiling-police-911 -living-while-black

Open Society Foundations, "Ethnic Profiling: What It Is and Why It Must End," May 2019. https://www.opensocietyfoundations.org /explainers/ethnic-profiling-what-it-and-why-it-must-end

Lynne Peeples, "What the Data Say About Police Brutality and Racial Bias—and Which Reforms Might Work," *Nature*, June 19, 2020. https://www.nature.com/articles/d41586-020-01846-z

Pierre Thomas, Yun Choi, Jasmine Brown, and Pete Madden, "Driving While Black: ABC News Analysis of Traffic Stops Reveals Racial Disparities in Several US Cities," ABC News, September 9, 2020. https://abcnews.go.com/US/driving-black -abc-news-analysis-traffic-stops-reveals/story?id=72891419

Liberty Vittert and Colby Dolly, "Measuring Racial Profiling: Why It's Hard to Tell Where Police Are Treating Minorities Unfairly," The Conversation, November 13, 2018. https://theconversation.com /measuring-racial-profiling-why-its-hard-to-tell-where-police -are-treating-minorities-unfairly-105455

OPPOSING
VIEWPOINTS®
SERIES

Chapter 2

Is the Court System Biased Against People of Color?

Chapter Preface

C ritics of US law enforcement and the justice system charge that racial profiling is an issue for many police officers. They also point to systemic, unfair sentencing once a suspect has been prosecuted. And statistics back up these claims.

The sheer number of incarcerations of African Americans for such minor offenses as marijuana possession and petty theft indicates inequity in the judicial system. Judges and juries seem to be willing to throw away Black lives for the same level of crimes for which white citizens are allowed to walk free, perhaps with just a slap on the wrist. Even conservative Republicans who have run on law-and-order platforms have recognized this imbalance and helped a generally impotent Congress to pass legislation that helped many people of color become unshackled by imprisonment.

The problem persists on all levels, however. Those who believe capital punishment should be abolished argue that not only are African American men more likely to be handed the death sentence, but they are also more likely to be wrongly accused of crimes that have supposedly warranted the ultimate punishment. For example, Curtis Flowers of Mississipi spent 23 years behind bars for murders he did not commit. Convicted on extremely weak evidence, he endured six trials tainted by racial discrimination and was sentenced to death four times before finally being exonerated. Even some who still feel that crimes such as murder justify the death penalty admit that Black males have not always been rightly sentenced.

This chapter cites the debate surrounding the American criminal justice system, not only pointing out its flaws but providing suggestions as to how it can be fixed. That "equal justice under the law" has been little more than a pie-in-the-sky motto for centuries in the United States is a given. Why racial inequality still exists and what must be done about it are the topics of discussion in chapter 2.

> *"A 2004 study found that when police officers were asked 'who looks criminal?' and shown a series of pictures, they more often chose black faces than white ones."*

Entrenched Racism Manifests in Disparate Treatment of Black Americans in the Criminal Justice System

Vera Institute of Justice

In the following viewpoint, the Vera Institute of Justice argues that the justice system treats African Americans unfairly compared to their white counterparts who commit crimes of similar levels. The author uses its own studies and statistical information to cite examples of how bias in law enforcement and in the court system have combined to destroy lives of those in poor communities for more than two centuries. The Vera Institute of Justice is an independent nonprofit research and policy organization that fights injustices in the criminal system.

"Research Confirms That Entrenched Racism Manifests in Disparate Treatment of Black Americans in Criminal Justice System," Vera Institute of Justice, May 3, 2018. Reprinted by permission.

As you read, consider the following questions:

1. How effectively does the author make its case of rampant racism in American courts?
2. What is the most alarming statistic used in this viewpoint regarding disparate treatment of African Americans by the justice system?
3. How has the war on drugs affected people of color?

Highly visible events—from Michael Brown in Ferguson, Missouri, to Eric Garner in Staten Island, New York; from Sandra Bland in Texas and Stephon Clark in California to Philando Castile in Minnesota—have served to elevate public awareness of disproportionate and unjustified police violence against black people. These tragic examples are representative of the disparities present in the justice system that undercut the life potential of people who live in communities of color.

The ways in which the criminal justice system operates to disadvantage black people are systemic and ingrained, and often subtle. A new evidence brief from the Vera Institute of Justice, *An Unjust Burden: The Disparate Treatment of Black Americans in the Criminal Justice System*, presents a summary of research demonstrating how America's history of racism and oppression continues to manifest in the criminal justice system and perpetuates the disparate treatment of black people. This evidence brief comes at a time when the conversation around our country's fraught history of violence and discrimination against black communities is receiving national attention.

"The racial disparities that exist at each and every juncture of the justice system are significant and indisputable. But the reasons behind these disparities are complex and demand deeper understanding," said Nicholas Turner, Executive Director of the Vera Institute of Justice. "They are rooted in a history of oppression and discriminatory decision making that has deliberately targeted black people; in a false and deceptive narrative of criminality; in implicit as well as conscious bias; in the legacy of structural racism and segregation. We believe that we must reckon with the deep body of evidence of bias that has caused black communities to become over-incarcerated, overpoliced, impoverished, and burdened with generational suffering. That's why this brief, which corrects the record, is so vital for this particular moment in time."

Some findings described and contextualized in *An Unjust Burden* include:

- Bias by decision makers at all stages of the justice process disadvantages black people. Studies have found that they are more likely to be stopped by the police, detained pretrial, charged with more serious crimes, and sentenced more harshly than white people. For example, a 2004 study found that when police officers were asked "who looks criminal?" and shown a series of pictures, they more often chose black faces than white ones. Also, a 2013 study found that federal prosecutors are more likely to charge black people than similarly situated white people with offenses that carry higher mandatory minimum sentences.
- The notion of "black on black crime"—recently invoked to counter #BlackLivesMatter protests of police shootings of black men by suggesting that the actual problem is black men shooting each other—is not borne out by statistics. A report from the Bureau of Justice Statistics found that most violence occurs between victims and offenders of the same race, regardless of race. The rate of both black-on-black and white-on-white nonfatal violence declined 79 percent between 1993 and 2015. The number of homicides involving both a black victim and black perpetrator fell from 7,361 in 1991 to 2,570 in 2016.
- Living in poor communities exposes people to risk factors for both offending and arrest, and a history of structural racism and inequality of opportunity—including de-

industrialization, red-lining, and white flight from neighborhoods—means that black people are more likely to be living in such conditions of concentrated poverty. Twenty-two percent of black people lived in poverty in 2016, compared to approximately 9 percent of white people. The widening reach of the criminal justice system in low-income communities of color further depletes resources and social capital in these places, perpetuating a tenacious cycle of poverty and criminal justice involvement.

- Discriminatory criminal justice policies and practices have historically and unjustifiably targeted black people since the Reconstruction Era to capitalize on a loophole in the 13th Amendment that states citizens cannot be enslaved unless convicted of a crime. Black Codes, vagrancy laws, and convict leasing were all used to continue post-slavery control over newly-freed people. The high arrest and incarceration rates of black Americans based on these racist policies deeply informed national discussions about racial differences that continue to this day. A 2010 study found that white Americans overestimate the share of burglaries, illegal drug sales, and juvenile crime committed by black people by approximately 20-30 percent.

- This discrimination continues today in often less overt ways, including through disparity in the enforcement of seemingly race-neutral laws. The "War on Drugs," for example, inspired policies like drug-free zones and habitual offender laws that produced differential outcomes by race. In Massachusetts, a 2004 review of sentencing data showed that black and Latino people accounted for 80 percent of drug-free zone convictions, even though 45 percent of those arrested statewide for drug offenses were white.

"Racism in the criminal justice system is inherent and undeniable," said Elizabeth Hinton, Assistant Professor in the Department of History and Department of African and African American Studies at Harvard University and lead author of

An Unjust Burden. "This brief illuminates the reasons why disproportionate numbers of black Americans are behind bars today, bringing together sociological, historical, and ethnographic data to help us better understand the root causes of racial disparities in the justice system."

> *"Blacks are also more likely than whites to see crime as a serious problem locally. In an early 2018 survey, black adults were roughly twice as likely as whites to say crime is a major problem in their local community (38% vs. 17%)."*

Black and White Americans Differ Widely in Their Views of the Criminal Justice System

John Gramlich

In the following viewpoint, John Gramlich cites widespread acknowledgement that people of color are far more likely to be treated unfairly by the American criminal justice system than their white counterparts, though he points out that the rate of understanding is far lower among white people. The author breaks down opinion research completed by the Pew Research Center into various categories, including policing in general, the death penalty and even voting rights among freed prisoners, as it cites unfairness in all aspects of criminal justice in the United States. John Gramlich is a senior writer and editor at the Pew Research Center.

"From Police to Parole, Black and White Americans Differ Widely in Their Views of Criminal Justice System," by John Gramlich, Pew Research Center, May 21, 2019.

As you read, consider the following questions:

1. What is the difference between Black and white Americans in terms of the percentage of people who believe the criminal justice system's treatment of minorities is a big problem?
2. What is a "feeling thermometer"?
3. Why do whites and Blacks have such differing opinions on the death penalty considering the latter is more concerned about crime in their communities?

B lack Americans are far more likely than whites to say the nation's criminal justice system is racially biased and that its treatment of minorities is a serious national problem.

In a recent Pew Research Center survey, around nine-in-ten black adults (87%) said blacks are generally treated less fairly by the criminal justice system than whites, a view shared by a much smaller majority of white adults (61%). And in a survey shortly before last year's midterm elections, 79% of blacks—compared with 32% of whites—said the way racial and ethnic minorities are treated by the criminal justice system is a very big problem in the United States today.

Racial differences in views of the criminal justice system are not limited to the perceived fairness of the system as a whole. Black and white adults also differ across a range of other criminal justice-related questions asked by the Center in recent years, on subjects ranging from crime and policing to the use of computer algorithms in parole decisions.

Here's an overview of these racial differences:

Crime

Black adults in the US consistently express more concern than white adults about crime.

In last year's preelection survey, three-quarters of blacks—compared with fewer than half of whites (46%)—said violent crime is a very big problem in the country today. And while 82% of blacks said gun violence is a very big problem in the US, just 47% of whites said the same.

Blacks are also more likely than whites to see crime as a serious problem locally. In an early 2018 survey, black adults were roughly twice as likely as whites to say crime is a major problem in their local community (38% vs. 17%).

That's consistent with a survey conducted in early 2017, when blacks were about twice as likely as whites to say their local community is not too or not at all safe from crime (34% vs. 15%). Black adults were also more likely than whites to say they worry a lot about having their home broken into (28% vs. 13%) or being the victim of a violent crime (20% vs. 8%). However, similar shares in both groups (22% of blacks and 18% of whites) said they actually had been the victim of a violent crime.

Policing

Some of the most pronounced differences between blacks and whites emerge on questions related to police officers and the work they do.

A survey conducted in mid-2017 asked Americans to rate police officers and other groups of people on a "feeling thermometer" from 0 to 100, where 0 represents the coldest, most negative rating and 100 represents the warmest and most positive. Black adults gave police officers a mean rating of 47; whites gave officers a mean rating of 72.

Blacks are also more likely than whites to have specific criticisms about the way officers do their jobs, particularly when it comes to police interactions with their community.

In the Center's survey earlier this year, 84% of black adults said that, in dealing with police, blacks are generally treated less fairly than whites. A much smaller share of whites—though still a 63% majority—said the same. Blacks were also about five times as likely as whites to say they'd been unfairly stopped by police because of their race or ethnicity (44% vs. 9%), with black men especially likely to say this (59%).

Stark racial differences about key aspects of policing also emerged in a 2016 survey. Blacks were much less likely than whites to say that police in their community do an excellent or good job using the right amount of force in each situation (33% vs. 75%), treating racial and ethnic groups equally (35% vs. 75%) and holding officers accountable when misconduct occurs (31% vs. 70%). Blacks were also substantially less likely than whites to say their local police do an excellent or good job at protecting people from crime (48% vs. 78%).

Notably, black-white differences in views of policing exist among officers themselves. In a survey of nearly 8,000 sworn officers conducted in the fall of 2016, black officers were about twice as likely as white officers (57% vs. 27%) to say that high-profile deaths of black people during encounters with police were signs of a broader problem, not isolated incidents. And roughly seven-in-ten black officers (69%)—compared with around a quarter of white officers (27%)—said the protests that followed many of these incidents were motivated some or a great deal by a genuine desire to hold police accountable for their actions, rather than by long-standing bias against the police. (Several other questions in the survey also showed stark differences in the views of black and white officers.)

The Death Penalty

A narrow majority of Americans (54%) support the death penalty for people convicted of murder, according to a spring 2018 survey. But only around a third of blacks (36%) support capital punishment for this crime, compared with nearly six-in-ten whites (59%).

Racial divisions extend to other questions related to the use of capital punishment. In a 2015 survey, 77% of blacks said minorities are more likely than whites to be sentenced to death for committing similar crimes. Whites were divided on this question: 46% said minorities are disproportionately sentenced to death, while the same percentage saw no racial disparities.

Blacks were also more likely than whites to say capital punishment is not a crime deterrent (75% vs. 60%) and were less likely to say the death penalty is morally justified (46% vs. 69%). However, about seven-in-ten in both groups said they saw some risk in putting an innocent person to death (74% of blacks vs. 70% of whites).

Parole Decisions

Certain aspects of the criminal justice system have changed in recent decades. One example: Some states now use criminal risk assessments to assist with parole decisions. These assessments involve collecting data about people who are up for parole, comparing that data with data about other people who have been convicted of crimes, and then assigning inmates a score to help decide whether they should be released from prison or not.

A 2018 survey asked Americans whether they felt the use of criminal risk assessments in parole decisions was an acceptable use of algorithmic decision-making. A 61% majority of black adults said using these assessments is unfair to people in parole hearings, compared with 49% of white adults.

Voting Rights for Ex-Felons

States differ widely when it comes to allowing people with past felony convictions to vote. In 12 states, people with certain felony convictions can lose the right to vote indefinitely unless other criteria—such as receiving a pardon from the governor—are met, according to the National Conference of State Legislatures. In Maine and Vermont, by contrast, those with felony convictions never lose the right to vote, even while they are incarcerated. Twenty-two states fall somewhere between these positions, rescinding voting rights only during incarceration and for a period afterward, such as when former inmates are on parole.

In a fall 2018 survey, 69% of Americans favored allowing people convicted of felonies to vote after serving their sentences. Black adults were much more likely than white adults to somewhat or strongly favor this approach (83% vs. 68%).

> *"A number of issues are at play that assure that most white-collar offenders will get off lightly; or not be caught at all."*

White-Collar Sentencing Is a Black Stain on America

Henry N. Pontell and Robert H. Tillman

In the following viewpoint, Henry N. Pontell and Robert H. Tillman argue that white-collar criminals get off lightly, compared with lower-status offenders. Their contentions were motivated by the weak sentencing of Paul Manafort, who committed white-collar crimes in his capacity as campaign chairman during Donald Trump's presidential campaign. The two authors also lambast the justice system for its unfairness regarding punishment for an alarming college admissions scandal that rocked the United States around the same time. Henry N. Pontell is a distinguished professor at John Jay College of Criminal Justice and professor emeritus at UC, Irvine. Robert H. Tillman is a professor at St. John's University. They are co-authors of Profit Without Honor: White-Collar Crime and the Looting of America.

As you read, consider the following questions:

1. Why do the authors express resentment about the Paul Manafort sentencing?
2. Are politically motivated white-collar crimes even more likely to result in lesser punishment than others?
3. Do presidents and others in power have the right to affect the sentencing of those who have helped or hindered their political careers?

The recent sentencing of Trump's former campaign chairman Paul Manafort demonstrates again that white-collar defendants in the American legal system get off lightly compared with their street counterparts.

The first sentence meted out to Manafort in Virginia would be seen as entirely misguided by almost all legal experts. Judge Ellis essentially trivialized the seriousness of the charges and politicized them in his fully biased and inappropriate remarks during the trial as due only to the special prosecutor's quest to get to Trump. The punishment amounted to nothing more than a slap on the wrist.

Manafort's second sentence in Washington DC given by a more measured jurist was still quite magnanimous given the charges, which included witness tampering, and was well under the maximum penalty of 10 years. Public outrage over the sentences is not surprising. A number of issues are at play that assure that most white-collar offenders will get off lightly; or not be caught at all.

First, consider that Paul Manafort, who the Virginia judge erroneously concluded led a "blameless life," would still be committing major financial frauds had he not put himself in the spotlight by volunteering to run Trump's campaign. Little did he know that he would end up in the crosshairs of a special prosecutor's investigation looking into Russian connections in the election, and even if he had thought of it, he might not have cared much. He had committed numerous major financial crimes, they were well-hidden, and he had cleverly avoided legal scrutiny in the past.

He had successfully played the limited capacity of the legal system to identify complex financial schemes, and to investigate and sanction them. Like others of his ilk, his illusion of invulnerability allowed him to commit major white-collar crimes with impunity. If he had not been in financial debt to Russian oligarchs, Manafort would not have had to volunteer as a campaign manager in order to sell political favors, and would likely never have come under any prosecutorial scrutiny at all.

Both sentences show the favorable results that can be attained by wealthy high-status defendants who can afford a bevy of very talented defense lawyers. Lower-end punishments can also be seen in relation to other less powerful white-collar offenders as well as to street criminals.

For example, simply compare Manfort's 7.5-year sentence to the Fyre Festival co-founder Billy McFarland's sentence of six years for what most would consider far less serious crimes regarding wire fraud, false ticket sales and misrepresentation. Even he was able to dodge a 15-year sentence sought by the prosecution. The sophisticated "starched" white-collar criminal fared practically the same as the music festival organizer who the judge referred to as a "serial fraudster." The same label could have applied to Manafort, only for more serious and costly offenses.

These results aren't entirely surprising. Criminological research demonstrates that white-collar defendants are likely to fare well compared with lower-status offenders. In a study of doctors convicted of fraud in California, for example, it was found that physicians were sanctioned significantly less than other first-time offenders who, on average, stole 10 times less. Similarly, during the savings and loan crisis a well-cited study showed that major financial fraudsters fared significantly better than federal offenders convicted of far less costly property crimes.

Public outrage at the sentences of powerful white-collar criminals such as Manafort more broadly indicates the normalization of such acts before the legal system, and highlights the need to understand the pernicious nature of the offenses and to take them more seriously. Since such crimes must be proactively policed by persons well-trained to do so, that means funding regulatory and policing agencies at much higher levels as well as

THE DEATH PENALTY

Few areas of criminal justice have sparked as much debate as the death penalty. The public strongly supports the death penalty even though there are strong arguments suggesting that it should be abolished.

Critics of capital punishment put forward several arguments.

1. The application of the death penalty is so arbitrary that it violates the Eighth Amendment's prohibition against cruel and unusual punishment. Justice Harry Blackmun claims there is an irreconcilable conflict between two requirements in capital sentencing. On the one hand, the Eighth Amendment demands that sentencing discretion in capital cases be structured according to fixed, objective standards to eliminate arbitrariness and discrimination. On the other hand, there is a humanitarian requirement that sentencing discretion be flexible enough to permit sentencers to individualize justice by taking mitigating circumstances into account that might justify a sentence less than death.
2. The death penalty discriminates against racial minorities and the poor. Statistics show that the death penalty is administered in a selective and racially discriminatory manner.
3. The death penalty doesn't deter crime.
4. The death penalty costs taxpayers more than life imprisonment.
5. The inevitability of factual, legal, and moral errors results in a system that must wrongly kill some innocent defendants.

sustained attention toward effective policies to induce compliance with the law.

Just a few days after Manafort was sentenced another national scandal emerged when the justice department charged 50 individuals for their participation in a college admissions cheating scam. Wealthy parents paid a consultant to bribe athletic coaches, falsify test scores and even submit doctored photos of

---

Proponents of the death penalty make arguments centering on the justifications of fairness, retribution, deterrence, economy, and popularity.

1. The death penalty isn't arbitrary. In *Gregg v. Georgia* (1976), the Supreme Court ruled that the death penalty isn't cruel and unusual punishment and that a two-part proceeding—one for determining innocence or guilt and one for determining the sentence—is constitutional. Any conflicts between eliminating arbitrariness and allowing sentencers to individualize justice can be resolved, according to Justice Scalia, by dispensing with the requirement that sentencers consider an array of mitigating circumstances.

2. The death penalty isn't discriminatory. In *McCleskey v. Kemp* (1987), the Court held that statistical evidence of racial discrimination in death sentencing can't establish a violation of the Eighth or Fourteenth Amendments. To win an appeal under the equal protection clause of the Fourteenth Amendment, the Court requires an appellant to prove the decision makers in his or her case acted with intent to discriminate.

3. Executions deter would-be criminals from committing crimes.

4. It is cheaper for the government to kill murderers than to keep them in prison for the duration of their lives.

"Should the Death Penalty Be Abolished?" Houghton Mifflin Harcourt.

---

their children's athletic bodies in order for them to gain admission to elite colleges and universities.

That scandal may seem less significant than Manafort's but has similar implications. Both cases, widely covered by the media, confirmed what many Americans had long suspected about the institutions that dominate our lives: that they are neither fair nor unbiased and favor the wealthy at every step.

> *"To many, capital punishment symbolizes justice and is the only way to adequately express society's revulsion of the murder of innocent lives."*

Is the Death Penalty Justified?

Chaya Benyamin

In the following viewpoint, Chaya Benyamin examines the pros and cons of the death penalty. The author cites those who believe the ultimate punishment must be meted out as a way to serve justice and protect innocent lives. But Benyamin also offers the other side of the coin, including assertions that the death penalty has never been determined to be a deterrent to crime and that the expense of holding prisoners for life precludes its worth. Benyamin ultimately leaves it up to the readers to decide for themselves with which view they agree. Chaya Benyamin is a writer, editor, and higher education professional.

As you read, consider the following questions:

1. What example does mobster Whitey Bulger serve?
2. What percentage of Americans support the death penalty?
3. What is the author's most persuasive point made against the death penalty?

"Is the Death Penalty Justified or Should It Be Abolished?" by Chaya Benyamin, Perspective-Media Ltd. Reprinted by permission.

Throughout history, societies around the world have used the death penalty as a way to punish the most heinous crimes. While capital punishment is still practiced today, many countries have since abolished it. In fact, in the US, California's governor recently put a moratorium on the death penalty, temporarily stopping it altogether. Given the moral complexities and depth of emotions involved, the death penalty remains a controversial debate the world over.

The following are three arguments in support of the death penalty and three against it.

Arguments Supporting the Death Penalty

Prevents Convicted Killers from Killing Again

The death penalty guarantees that convicted murderers will never kill again. There have been countless cases where convicts sentenced to life in prison have murdered other inmates and/or prison guards. Convicts have also been known to successfully arrange murders from within prison, the most famous case being mobster Whitey Bulger, who apparently was killed by fellow inmates while incarcerated. There are also cases where convicts who have been released for parole after serving only part of their sentences—even life sentences—have murdered again after returning to society. A death sentence is the only irrevocable penalty that protects innocent lives.

Maintains Justice

For most people, life is sacred and innocent lives should be valued over the lives of killers. Innocent victims who have been murdered—and in some cases, tortured beforehand—had no choice in their untimely and cruel death or any opportunity to say goodbye to friends and family, prepare wills, or enjoy their last moments of life. Meanwhile, convicted murderers sentenced to life in prison—and even those on death row—are still able to learn, read, write, paint, find religion, watch TV, listen to music, maintain relationships, and even appeal their sentence.

To many, capital punishment symbolizes justice and is the only way to adequately express society's revulsion of the murder of innocent lives. According to a 2018 Gallup Poll, the majority of Americans (55%) think that legal executions fit the crime of what convicted killers deserve. The death penalty is a way to restore society's balance of justice—by showing that the most severe crimes are intolerable and will be punished in kind.

Historically Recognized

Historians and constitutional lawyers seem to agree that by the time the Founding Fathers wrote and signed the US Constitution in 1787, and when the Bill of Rights were ratified and added in 1791, the death penalty was an acceptable and permissible form of punishment for premeditated murder.

The Constitution's 8th and 14th Amendments recognize the death penalty BUT under due process of the law. This means that certain legal requirements must first be fulfilled before any state executions can be legally carried out—even when pertaining to the cruelest, most cold-blooded murderer. While interpretations of the amendments pertaining to the death penalty have changed over the years, the Founding Fathers intended to allow for the death penalty from the very beginning and put in place a legal system to ensure due process.

Arguments Against the Death Penalty

Not Proven to Deter Crime

There's no concrete evidence showing that the death penalty actually deters crime. Various studies comparing crime and murder rates in US states that have the death penalty versus those that don't found very little difference between the two. These inconclusive findings mean that capital punishment may or may not be a deterrent for crime. No definitive answer is reason enough to abolish it.

More Expensive Than Imprisonment

Contrary to popular belief, the death penalty is actually more expensive than keeping an inmate in prison, even for life. While the cost of the actual execution may be minimal, the overall costs surrounding a capital case (where the death penalty is a potential punishment) are enormously high. Sources say that defending a death penalty case can cost around four times higher than defending a case not seeking death. Even in cases where a guilty plea cancels out the need for a trial, seeking the death penalty costs almost twice as much as cases that don't. And this is before factoring in appeals, which are more time-consuming and therefore cost more than life-sentence appeals, as well as higher prison costs for death-row inmates.

Does Not Bring Closure

It seems logical that punishing a murderer or terrorist with the most severe punishment would bring closure and relief to victims' families. However, the opposite seems to be true. Studies show that capital punishment does not bring comfort to those affected by violent and fatal crimes. In fact, punishing the perpetrator has been shown to make victims feel worse, as it forces them to think about the offender and the incident even more. Also, as capital cases can drag on for years due to endless court appeals, it can be difficult for victims' families to heal, thus delaying closure.

The Bottom Line

The death penalty has been used to maintain the balance of justice throughout history, punishing violent criminals in the severest way to ensure they won't kill again. On the other hand, with inconclusive evidence as to its deterrence of crime, the higher costs involved in pursuing capital cases, and the lack of relief and closure it brings to victims' families, the death penalty is not justified. Where do you stand on this controversial issue?

> *"The death penalty traumatizes
> everyone it touches: victim survivors,
> prosecutors, defense lawyers, prison
> workers and families."*

The Death Penalty Should Be Abolished

Diann Rust-Tierney

In the following viewpoint, Diann Rust-Tierney argues that capital punishment has not proven itself to be a deterrent to crime, has not been sentenced fairly to all people throughout the United States, and does not address the root causes of crime, such as issues involving mental health, education, housing, and steady and fruitful employment opportunities. Though the families of victims of crimes that carry the death penalty might not agree, many believe her points have merit. Diann Rust-Tierney is the executive director for the National Coalition to Abolish the Death Penalty.

As you read, consider the following questions:

1. Who are some of the victims of capital punishment aside from those put to death?
2. What does a declining death penalty rate mean?
3. Should the death penalty be judged on the severity of the crime?

D espite the shocking spectacle of assembly-line executions in Arkansas earlier this year, the use of the death penalty is in decline. Arkansas's willingness to execute four men in eight days, including two in a single night, demonstrates the extreme lengths to which proponents of capital punishment will go to retain this brutal practice—and why it must be abolished.

The death penalty is now largely isolated to only a small handful of states which actively use it, but despite this diminished use, the flaws and failures of capital punishment are more apparent than ever.

The Death Penalty Does Not Improve Public Safety

We all want a criminal justice system that's sensible, effective, and creates a safe society with less crime—and evidence shows that the death penalty has no impact on public safety. Stats from the Death Penalty Information Center indicate that in the past forty years, there have been 1,184 executions in the South compared to just four in the Northeast, and yet homicide figures in 2015 were nearly 70 percent higher in the Southern states.

We need to take a closer look at what works and what doesn't, and use a common-sense approach to improve public safety. By abolishing the death penalty, we could focus our time, energy and resources on supporting victims and families harmed by violence. We must ensure that all victims are treated fairly and with respect. If you listen to victims speak about their experience with the death penalty, you find that virtually all are frustrated with the current system. There's no such thing as quick and easy in a system that's supposed to be deliberative to ensure that the innocent aren't punished along with the guilty—and even then the system gets it wrong too often.

Moreover, all victims are not treated fairly. Survivors of homicide who oppose the death penalty report being treated like second-class victims by some prosecutors. Questions about the death penalty divide families needlessly. Further, there are stark disparities in how victims are treated based on race. A study by

Fairness in the Criminal Justice System

Everyone wants the criminal justice system to be fair. Why then is there so much controversy about fairness? One important reason is lack of clarity about what fairness means. Even when clear conceptions of fairness are provided, there can be several different kinds that are in conflict. For example, men are vastly overrepresented in prisons compared to women. On its face, this is an instance of unfairness in outcome. The chances a judge will sentence a man to prison are far greater than the chances a judge will sentence a woman to prison. One reason is that men are far more likely to be convicted of violent crimes for which a long prison sentence is expected.

The overrepresentation of men in prison could be easily remedied. One could decide to treat men and women differently. One could stipulate that violent crimes committed by men were less serious than violent crimes committed by women and that, therefore, incarceration was less appropriate. This would increase fairness in outcome while decreasing fairness in treatment.

Would such a tradeoff be accepted? A lot would depend on why men are more likely than women to be are arrested for, charged with, and convicted of violent crimes. If in fact men were no more likely than women to commit violent crimes to begin with, and if the overrepresentation of men among those arrested for, charged with, and convicted of violent crimes derived from a bias again men, the tradeoff might be accepted. But that just moves concerns about fairness upstream, where the same two tradeoffs would need to be addressed at each stage. At some point, fairness upstream would need to be examined in settings and institutions well before an arrest for a violent crime occurs. For example, why are boys more likely to be disciplined in school?

At each stage, there would be a need for data and a proper analysis so that facts could be accumulated. Are men in a given jurisdiction more likely than women to be stopped and questioned by police? If so, why is that? And might some of the reasons have a legitimate law enforcement rationale? Facts matter. Do men constitute the majority of arrests in intimate partner violence? If so, why? And might some of the reasons have a legitimate law enforcement rationale? Again, facts matter.

"Fairness in the Criminal Justice System," by Richard Berk, Trustees of the University of Pennsylvania School of Arts & Sciences, September 28, 2017.

the Vera Institute in 2014 found that victim assistance services including treatment for trauma are routinely unavailable to young African American men. Despite their ordeal, the system is more likely to treat African American men as perpetrators or even complicit in their victimization. We need to take the focus, attention and resources that the death penalty steals to focus our hearts and hands on creating a culture of healing and support for victims of homicide and violence.

The Death Penalty Does Not Address the Root Causes of Crime

Our focus needs to be on preventing crime and violence. We know that to reduce crime and violence we must focus on the root causes of crime. Crime happens when other issues are neglected such as mental health, housing, access to education and sustainable employment options. When these issues are addressed, communities become safe and vibrant, and when you look at those on death row in the United States, you see the costly evidence of neglecting children, families and communities at risk. We can help move communities and our nation forward by addressing the root causes of crime to create strong, healthy families and our communities.

Most law enforcement officials agree that the death penalty is not a deterrent to crime. Perpetrators rarely consider the consequences when they engage in violence—if they did they wouldn't commit crimes in the first place. The few people who might think about the consequences also think they won't get caught, so the death penalty isn't a factor.

These same people rank the death penalty last among their priorities for crime reduction. We already know that executions have no impact in reducing crime, so shouldn't we get ahead of the problem? Shouldn't we provide positive interventions for people and communities at risk? A brutal execution in the middle of the night won't prevent the next tragedy.

The Death Penalty Is Not Applied Fairly Across the Country

In 2016, 30 death sentences were imposed across the United States, making it the lowest number in 40 years. In fact, the death penalty is in decline by every measure; only 20 executions took place last year and just four states, Georgia, Texas, Florida and Missouri, were responsible for 90 percent of them. The death penalty has also been eliminated in six states and four more states have put a moratorium on executions. Overall, only a handful of counties (just two percent) impose death sentences in the US.

As use of the death penalty declines, we must pay attention to those who are selected for this severe punishment. Being sentenced to death doesn't depend on whether you've committed the worst crime, but where the crime is committed. People who live in the South are more likely to receive death sentences than people in other parts of the country—even when they commit the same crime. One of the reasons that the death penalty is used more in the South is because these states are notorious for failing to provide public defenders to those who can't afford one, even though the Constitution requires them to do so. And, often, whether you're sentenced to death or not depends on whether you had a good lawyer.

Issues of racial inequality also continue to plague our criminal justice system. Activists challenging police shootings of unarmed African American men and the disparate treatment of victims based on race provide modern day examples of the way in which racial bias continues to infect our justice system, including the death penalty. While we strive to address these problems, the best way to make sure that there's fairness is to abolish the death penalty in all states.

We Can Change

We're all more than the worst thing we've ever done, because all human beings are capable of change. If our criminal justice system is to change, it should be designed not just to punish, but to also rehabilitate those who've committed crimes. There should always be the opportunity for rehabilitation, redemption and grace. We have the capacity to hold people accountable and separate dangerous people from society without foreclosing that opportunity.

So, do we continue down a path that has failed repeatedly to produce results? Do we continue with an institution that inflicts harm? The death penalty traumatizes everyone it touches: victim survivors, prosecutors, defense lawyers, prison workers and families. Former wardens, guards and execution team members report severe damage to their mental and physical health because of the stress and trauma of participating in executions and killing prisoners. It doesn't have to be this way. The death penalty is an old-fashioned, outdated, harmful practice, and it must be abolished.

Periodical and Internet Sources Bibliography

The following articles have been selected to supplement the diverse views presented in this chapter.

Alliance for Justice, "Batson's Unfulfilled Promise: Curtis Flowers and Racial Exclusion in the Jury Selection Process," April 30, 2019. https://www.afj.org/article/batsons-unfulfilled-promise-curtis -flowers-and-racial-exclusion-in-the-jury-selection-process/

Melissa Brown and Rashawn Ray, "Breonna Taylor, Police Brutality, and the Importance of #SayHerName," Brookings, September 25, 2020. https://www.brookings.edu/blog/how-we-rise/2020/09/25 /breonna-taylor-police-brutality-and-the-importance-of -sayhername

Steve Dubb, "Case of Breonna Taylor Shines Light on Structural Racism in US Justice System," *Nonprofit Quarterly*, September 28, 2020. https://nonprofitquarterly.org/case-of-breonna-taylor -shines-light-on-structural-racism-in-us-justice-system

Tara Eaves, "Letters: The United States Should Keep the Death Penalty," *The Advocate*, September 30, 2019. https://www .theadvocate.com/baton_rouge/opinion/letters/article_070493e8 -e39f-11e9-aad2-dffc95387147.html

Matt Ford, "Racism and the Execution Chamber," *The Atlantic*, June 23, 2014. https://www.theatlantic.com/politics/archive/2014/06 /race-and-the-death-penalty/373081/

Kwadwo Frimpong, "Black People Are Still Seeking Racial Justice— Why and What to Do About It," Brookings, November 11, 2020. https://www.brookings.edu/blog/how-we-rise/2020/11/12/black -people-are-still-seeking-racial-justice-why-and-what-to-do -about-it/

Innovations for Poverty Action, "Discrimination in the Judicial System." https://www.poverty-action.org/study/discrimination -judicial-system

Adam Liptak, "A Vast Racial Gap in Death Penalty Cases, New Study Finds," *New York Times*, August 3, 2020. https://www.nytimes .com/2020/08/03/us/racial-gap-death-penalty.html

Louis Menand, "The Supreme Court Case That Enshrined White Supremacy in Law," *New Yorker*, January 28, 2019. https://www .newyorker.com/magazine/2019/02/04/the-supreme-court-case -that-enshrined-white-supremacy-in-law

Kailey Morgan, "Even on Death Row, There's No Escape from Racism and Discrimination for Black Women," NC Policy Watch, February 11, 2021. http://www.ncpolicywatch.com/2021/02/11 /even-on-death-row-theres-no-escape-from-racism-and -discrimination-for-black-women/

NPR, "The New Science Behind Our 'Unfair' Criminal Justice System," July 6, 2015. https://www.npr .org/2015/07/06/418585084/the-new-science-behind -our-unfair-criminal-justice-system

Ana Swanson, "The US Court System Is Criminally Unjust," *Washington Post*, July 20, 2015. https://www.washingtonpost .com/news/wonk/wp/2015/07/20/why-the-u-s-court-system-is -criminally-unjust/

Vangela M. Wade, "Curtis Flowers Will Finally Be Freed. Prosecutorial Misconduct Remains a Problem," *Washington Post*, September 6, 2020. https://www.washingtonpost.com /opinions/2020/09/06/curtis-flowers-will-finally-be-freed -prosecutorial-misconduct-remains-problem

OPPOSING
VIEWPOINTS®
SERIES

CHAPTER 3

Would Changing Laws Change Outcomes?

Chapter Preface

It is easier to point out examples of the historical and current contentious relationship between law enforcement and African Americans than it is to offer viable solutions. There is much gray area in that relationship and in all suggestions, however well intentioned. The notion that anything can be done to completely solve the problem might be considered ludicrous. But any perception that there is little that can be done to promote healthier relations between the police and Black Americans is likely more outlandish.

Previous attempts to reduce criminal activity have driven a wedge between law enforcement and some of the communities they police. Policies such as stop-and-frisk have served to target and alienate the Black and Latino communities. This chapter features viewpoints that offer both positive and negative assessments of stop-and-frisk laws, but what has become apparent in recent history is that they are fading away as a viable alternative.

What has grown more obvious in the spate of police shootings, mistreatment, and killings of African Americans is that the methods of policing in poor inner city communities has been largely ineffective and combative. Some long for what they perceive as the "good old days" during which police officers patrolled on foot and became pillars of the communities in which they worked, even friends to those they served. While some might consider that a more dangerous approach, the notion of law enforcement officials getting to know people personally and gaining trust has certainly been considered more viable than current policing methods.

This chapter explores stop-and-frisk, comparing issues such as drug addiction in prevalently white and black communities, and ideas for more positive and creative approaches to policing poor neighborhoods.

> *"Trump has claimed he wants to help Black and Latino communities, but for them, policies like stop-and-frisk are a total disaster. Instead of making cities safer, a return to stop-and-frisk is far more likely to produce thousands of forceful and terrifying experiences with police."*

Put an End to Stop-and-Frisk

Rose Lenehan

In the following viewpoint, Rose Lenehan argues that stop-and-frisk methods of policing are discriminatory. Stop-and-frisk has been roundly criticized and even has been abolished in some communities. The author cites statistics suggesting that targets of stop-and-frisk have been skewed greatly against African American and Latino suspects. Rose Lenehan is a PhD candidate in philosophy at Massachusetts Institute of Technology and a member of the Young Professionals Network of the Prison Policy Initiative, a nonprofit organization that seeks to expose the harm of mass criminalization and spark advocacy campaigns to create a more just society.

"What 'Stop-and-Frisk' Really Means: Discrimination & Use of Force," by Rose Lenehan, Prison Policy Initiative, August 17, 2017. Reprinted by permission.

As you read, consider the following questions:

1. What president supported stop-and-frisk, even after the practice was summarily criticized?
2. How much more often were NYPD officers found to use force against Black suspects versus white suspects?
3. What do statistics show about how different races trust the police?

I would do stop-and-frisk. I see what's going on here, I see what's going on in Chicago, I think stop-and-frisk. In New York City it was so incredible, the way it worked.

—Donald Trump,
September 2016

P resident Donald Trump has expressed support for stop-and-frisk repeatedly, even before he endorsed the practice as a presidential candidate. But he's wrong: stop and frisk does not work. While it was policy in New York, the crime rate declined—but it also declined in many other cities that sensibly avoided stopping citizens without good reason: Los Angeles, Atlanta, Dallas, and San Diego.

The question of whether a policy like stop-and-frisk is effective is moot if it systematically violates citizens' rights. As a federal judge pointed out in the 2013 case against stop-and-frisk in New York City, "Many police practices may be useful for fighting crime— preventive detention or coerced confession, for example—but because they are unconstitutional *they cannot be used*, no matter how effective" [emphasis added]. The judge found that stop-and-frisk in New York City had been racially discriminatory, violating both the Fourth Amendment and the equal protection clause of the 14th Amendment.

By now it's well known that stop-and-frisk disproportionately targets Black and Latino communities. But the policy is even more destructive than you think. To see how stop-and-frisk was implemented, we looked at the raw NYPD data on stop-and-frisk in 2011. That was the peak year for stop-and-frisk in New York City, when police made 685,724 stops—almost 2,000 stops every single day. Our analysis shows that the police used physical force in almost a quarter of stops—and that their use of force is also racially discriminatory.

In 2011, the police stopped Black and Latino people 574,483 times and used physical force against them almost 130,000 times. "Physical force" includes pushing people to the ground, forcing them against a wall or a car, pointing guns at them, and using batons or pepper spray. The police reported using force in 23% of stops of Blacks and Latinos, but in only 16% of stops of Whites. And for what? The police found weapons—mostly knives—in about 1% of stops of Blacks and Latinos. They found weapons on Whites they stopped nearly twice as often.

The police seem to employ very different thresholds of suspicion when deciding to stop Blacks and Latinos versus Whites. Three data points support this conclusion. First are the differing success rates: Officers are more likely to arrest Whites they stop and more likely to find a weapon. Second, a higher proportion of stops of Whites originate in radio calls, meaning the stop isn't entirely a matter of the officer's discretion. Third is the difference in the reasons given for the stop. Anytime officers stop someone, they have to report the reason for the stop, choosing from among several options.

The most commonly cited rationale is "furtive movements," which could mean almost anything. Officers testifying in *Floyd v. City of New York* gave examples like "walking in a certain way" and "changing direction." Unsurprisingly, "furtive movements" was more often cited as the reason for the stop for Blacks and Latinos than for Whites. This all suggests that when officers are

GANG VIOLENCE

The ongoing state and Trump administration crackdown against MS-13 in one of their most infamous strongholds has taken such a toll on the gang that they've only been linked to a single murder in the area during 2018.

Police in Long Island—a part of New York that has been a hotbed for violent crime at the hands of MS-13—told *Newsday* that four homicides recorded there in 2018 appeared to be linked to the gang, down from 14 the year prior. Yet only one of those murders is said to have occurred this year. The other three cases were killings believed to have happened in 2015 and 2017, but they were counted in 2018 totals since the bodies were found within the past 12 months.

"Suffolk County has waged war against MS-13 and our comprehensive strategy to eradicate this violent gang from Long Island is working," Suffolk County Executive Steve Bellone told Fox News in a statement Monday. "This dramatic reduction is a result of great policing, expanded community outreach and leveraging governmental partnerships to bring in additional resources to combat gang violence."

dealing with White people their police work is much more careful. It apparently takes a lot less for an officer to consider Black or Latino people "suspicious."

The racial disparities inherent in policies like stop-and-frisk help explain why different racial groups see the police differently. According to a Pew study from September 2016, 75% of Whites but only 33% of Blacks believe the police use the right amount of force for each situation. 75% of Whites but only 35% of Blacks believe police treat racial and ethnic groups equally. 42% of Whites but only 14% of Blacks say they have a lot of confidence in the police department in their community. When people don't trust the police, they don't assist them, they don't report crime, and they don't call for help.

Six of the 14 homicides on Long Island last year connected to MS-13 happened in Suffolk County, according to *Newsday*.

The one murder MS-13 is suspected to have committed on Long Island this year happened just days ago, on Dec. 18 in Nassau County. The body of Harold Sermeno, a 17-year-old, was found in a picnic area behind a community center near Lawrence, a village that borders New York City. Investigators say Sermeno was shot multiple times.

Officials reportedly believe his murder is tied to the Dec. 22 killing of Ian Michel Cruz, who was found dead in a park in Far Rockaway, a neighborhood adjacent to Lawrence and within the New York City limits. Five people were arrested following the death of Cruz, who also was shot multiple times. Police suspect both men were lured to the parks with the promise of sex, according to the *Long Island Herald.*

Trump, in a visit to Long Island last summer, vowed to "liberate our towns" from MS-13's grip, and he has a made a crackdown on the gang one of the focal points of his administration.

"We will find you, we will arrest you, we will jail you and we will deport you," Trump has said, garnering applause from an audience of law enforcement officials.

"MS-13 Crackdown Severely Reduces Gang's Violent Criminal Activity in New York Stronghold," by Greg Norman, FOX News Network, LLC, December 31, 2018.

Trump has claimed he wants to help Black and Latino communities, but for them, policies like stop-and-frisk are a total disaster. Instead of making cities safer, a return to stop-and-frisk is far more likely to produce thousands of forceful and terrifying experiences with police, as well as create and exacerbate distrust of the police within communities they are supposed to be serving.

> *"Officers can be fair to suspects if they stop and question a person only when objective circumstances give rise to reasonable suspicion of criminal activity—and if they frisk that person only when clear facts suggest the person may be armed."*

Stop-and-Frisk Can Work

Henry F. Fradella and Michael D. White

In the following viewpoint, Henry F. Fradella and Michael D. White argue that the stop-and-frisk policy of policing can work if it is practiced fairly and carefully and if people are treated with respect. The authors use statistical information that shows such treatment has not always been provided by law enforcement officials. But the authors maintain that stop-and-frisk can be a deterrent to crime if carried out properly. Henry F. Fradella is a professor and associate director of criminology and criminal justice at Arizona State University. Michael D. White is a professsor of criminology and criminal justice at Arizona State University.

As you read, consider the following questions:

1. According to the authors, can most police officers be trusted to be objective and fair when selecting suspects to stop and frisk?
2. What is the significance of the Supreme Court case *Terry v. Ohio*?
3. Why have inner-city communities been the most vocal critics of stop-and-frisk policies?

In mid-November, former New York City Mayor Michael Bloomberg apologized publicly for his backing of a practice intended to reduce violent crime that had for years been criticized as racially biased. "I realize back then I was wrong, and I'm sorry," he said.

But his apology, made at a predominantly black church in Brooklyn, puzzled many observers. That included scholars of criminal justice like ourselves.

Bloomberg has long been a vocal supporter of a policy the city police department officially called "Stop, Question, and Frisk," including during his time as New York's mayor. In an effort to control crime, police aggressively and indiscriminately stopped and questioned people on the streets or in public housing projects. Police also often patted down suspects to check for weapons.

His apology was confusing because that phrase, often shortened to "stop and frisk," is used to describe two different things.

As we wrote in our book, *Stop and Frisk: The Use and Abuse of a Controversial Policing Tactic*, one is a legitimate, constitutionally sanctioned tactic, grounded in a police officer's reasonable suspicion that a particular person is engaged in criminal activity.

The other is an illegitimate, broad crime-control strategy that, more often than not, ignores the law's requirement that a particular person be reasonably suspected of breaking the law.

A Legal Tactic

For centuries, the English common law tradition, which undergirds US law, has recognized a police officer's right to stop a member of the public to inquire about potentially criminal behavior. They can do this without needing to meet the legal standard for arresting the person and charging them with a crime—provided the officer had reasonable grounds to be suspicious in the first place.

In 1968, the US Supreme Court codified that practice in its decision in *Terry v. Ohio*. In that case, a police officer saw two black men walking up and down a Cleveland street and repeatedly peering into a particular store's windows. A white man joined them, after which the police officer approached the group, identified himself and patted down the men's clothes—effectively, stopping and frisking them. The pat-down revealed that two of them were carrying illegally concealed firearms and burglars' tools.

The men challenged the constitutionality of the initial stop and the subsequent pat-down. When the case got to the Supreme Court, the justices established that stop-and-frisk was a practice fundamentally different than a search or seizure as specified by the Fourth Amendment. They concluded that the police officer had what they called a "reasonable suspicion" that the suspects were preparing to burglarize the store.

The court also ruled that police could pat down suspects to ensure they aren't armed with weapons that could be used against the officers.

Taken together, the ruling gives police broad authority to decide when, whether and why to stop, question and frisk people.

In several rulings since 1968, the Supreme Court has expanded officers' power to stop members of the public. That expanded power includes stopping someone in the open concourse area of an airport and requesting to see person's ticket and identification, briefly searching a car for hidden weapons, stopping people for minor infractions while really investigating more serious crimes and even frisking people under the pretext of looking for weapons in hopes of finding drugs.

Left unchecked, all that discretion could lead to discriminatory, racially unjust and unconstitutional behavior in which blacks and Hispanics are targeted more often than their proportion of the population would suggest they should be.

A Broad Strategy

At its core, the stop-and-frisk approach is supposed to rely on more than a hunch. But the low burden of proof, the large discretion granted to police and the relatively invisible nature of these sorts of encounters combine to create real potential for abuse. Indeed, several US police departments turned stop-and-frisk tactics into a wider, more aggressive strategy to cut down on crime.

Since 2002, New York City police officers, for instance, have stopped, questioned and often frisked hundreds of thousands of people each year. Police conducted more than 685,000 stops in 2011 alone. Over 82% of the people stopped were black or Hispanic, in a city where 52% of the population is black or Hispanic. Just 12% of all stops—of people of any race—resulted in an arrest or a summons.

Based on that data, a federal judge ruled in 2013 that the New York Police Department had unconstitutionally racially profiled its stop-and-frisk targets.

That year, New York police stopped 191,851 people; since 2014, under Bloomberg's successor Mayor Bill DeBlasio, the number has dropped steadily. In 2018, just 11,008 people were stopped, and 31% of the stops resulted in an arrest or a summons.

Taking On Crime

New York's aggressive stopping-and-frisking practices happened at the same time as changes within the city's police department, including a strategy in which police commanders identified what they called "high-crime areas" and flooded those locations with officers on foot patrols.

During that same time frame, the city's crime rate dropped—especially its murder rate.

But crime rates stayed historically low even after officers dramatically reduced the frequency of stop-and-frisk encounters, signaling that other circumstances—not stop-and-frisk—drove the crime rate lower.

A Path Forward, with Caution

Despite those problems in New York, we believe that it is possible for stop-and-frisk to succeed in contemporary policing—so long as it is not used broadly and indiscriminately.

Officers can be fair to suspects if they stop and question a person only when objective circumstances give rise to reasonable suspicion of criminal activity—and if they frisk that person only when clear facts suggest the person may be armed.

For instance, it could be appropriate for an officer to stop and frisk someone on the street for wearing a trench coat in hot weather. Another example that could warrant a stop-and-frisk would be if an officer sees someone repeatedly entering and leaving a bank or store without doing any business inside.

Those situations don't depend on the race or ethnicity of the potential suspect. Racial or ethnic characteristics should be part of an officer's decision to stop someone only if the person in other ways matches a description of a criminal suspect police are seeking.

Given the pervasiveness of racism and implicit bias, we believe that police departments that use stop-and-frisk tactics should be actively on guard against officers' misuse of police power.

That includes careful recruitment and selection of new officers, excellent training and clearly written policies. Moreover, officers must be supervised in ways that increase accountability and transparency, potentially involving external oversight.

Body-worn cameras offer an opportunity for police departments to monitor and control officer decision-making during stop-and-frisk activities. Supervisors, training officers and even community members could systematically review body-worn camera footage as part of efforts to hold officers accountable for staying within the bounds of department policies and constitutional limitations.

If used properly, we believe, stop-and-frisk can be successfully and legitimately used while treating people with dignity and respect and giving suspects fair opportunities to tell their sides of the story. By making decisions fairly and acting with trustworthy motives, officers can ensure public safety while honoring citizens' constitutional rights.

"When drug users were thought to be
predominantly black, punishments
were often severe. Now that the
spread of heroin has changed, and is
better understood, the entire context
of the situation is looked at in a
different light."

Now That Drugs Have Infiltrated White Communities, Laws May Change

American Addiction Centers

*In the following viewpoint, American Addiction Centers refutes the
notion that drug addiction is generally a problem most associated
with inner-city communities and people from poorer backgrounds.
The author discusses the scourge of addiction in America's rural,
suburban, and urban areas and shows that the problem is not
concentrated anywhere in particular and, troublingly, has grown
among those in a wide age range. American Addiction Centers works
to provide evidence-based treatment for addictions and mental health
care throughout the United States.*

"Comparing Substance Abuse in Urban, Suburban, and Rural America," American
Addiction Centers. Reprinted by permission.

As you read, consider the following questions:

1. Why do some people believe heroin addiction is only a major problem in inner cities?
2. What is "hillbilly heroin"?
3. What conditions in America have allowed heroin addiction to become so widespread in recent years?

D rug addiction has spread its tentacles across the United States comprehensively and deeply as a threat to public health. For generations, it was thought that only "some people" in "some places" would use drugs; but as numbers and maps have shown, there is no city, region, or state that has not struggled with the insidious spread of illicit substances. Comparing substance abuse in urban, suburban, and rural America shows the full scope of the drug problem in America and may offer solutions on how to address the issue.

The Heroin Problem of Berks County

There are many millions of stories from communities across the country about how drugs have killed children, torn apart families, and prematurely ended hopes and dreams. One of those stories comes from Berks County in southeastern Pennsylvania. With quaint farmland and stone barns constructed in the 19th century, NPR writes that everyone knows everyone in this rural area of 411,000 people.[1]

It sounds perfect, but "opioid addiction is deeply embedded" in small towns like Kutztown, Pennsylvania (population 5,012 in 2010). A paramedic talking to NPR explains that since heroin is cheap and easily obtainable from big cities (such as nearby Reading and Philadelphia), "there is no exclusive demographic" that has been affected. People from all demographics—from youths to adults, low-income to high-income people—have fallen under the sway.

Over a period of two years, two high schools in the area had to bury six students who overdosed on heroin.

In response, the community of Berks County has come together to raise awareness about opioid addiction—not just black tar heroin, but the prescription pills that are crushed and snorted; just consumed en masse by people who have chronic pain or who have a mental health illness that compels them to abuse drugs; or for any number of other reasons that have led to painkillers becoming the most widely abused drugs in America today.

"Heroin Is Everywhere"

Such is the prevalence of narcotics that heroin no longer has the stigma that once kept impressionable and impulsive teenagers far away from it. A guidance counselor explains that the availability and affordability of heroin overrides negative perceptions of the substance: No longer is heroin that something only junkies do in the depths of their depression. Now, heroin is everywhere.

And NPR explains that in a small town like Kutztown, boredom sets in quickly. Local efforts have included outdoor movie nights, line dancing nights, and other activities to ensure that drugs do not fill the void in teenagers' lives.[2]

Even when problems are identified early and students are enrolled in treatment and rehabilitation programs, rural areas like Kutztown and Berks County do not offer many safe havens; following their discharge, students will most likely return to the same circle of friends, the same home environments, and the same cues, triggers, and temptations that set the scene for their initial dalliance with heroin.

Hillbilly Heroin

The substance abuse problems facing a rural region like Kutztown are felt across small towns and counties across the country, but particularly in New England and the Northeast. Such areas pride themselves on their fierce independence from the big metropolitan cities in their states, hearkening back to days of being in the wild frontier of a simpler America. *Rice and Bread* magazines writes of how the practice of making moonshine across the Appalachians—and snubbing the Bureau of Alcohol, Tobacco, Firearms and Explosives—is a cultural legacy.[3]

But this has also created a sense of isolation that feeds into the spell of drugs like heroin. It has further led to an environment where residents do not trust local government to look after their interests, where law enforcement—what little there is—responds too slowly to signs of abuse, and emergency medical services cannot intervene in time to save a life.

The situation has created a destination for drug traffickers, who exploit the vulnerable populations of the rural towns of industrial and farming states like Kentucky, Virginia, and West Virginia. While the rest of the world uses terms like *opioid epidemic* and *opioid crisis*, it's given a different name on the small towns and streets where the disease spreads: hillbilly heroin. The victims are usually poor, poorly educated, and prone to workplace injuries due to the physical nature of their work. Once introduced to medication, they are fed a poisoned lifeline of OxyContin and other prescriptions to keep them coming back (until they overdose). In 2001, the *Guardian* reported that 40 percent of adults in the region were dependent on opioids.[4]

In Kermit, West Virginia (total area 0.39 square miles, population 406), the former Sav-Rite pharmacy distributed prescription drugs to customers without checking for prescriptions. That location, and another one 10 miles away, handed out almost 3.2 million units of hydrocodone (an opioid pain medication that is sold as Vicodin) in 2006. At the time, the national average was 97,000. *Salon* magazine called Kermit "America's pill-popping capital" and the epicenter of the prescription drug epidemic.[5]

Looking for Answers

Rural America is treasured for its bucolic setting, but in his 2014 State of the State address to the Vermont legislature, Governor Peter Shumlin devoted his entire speech to talking about the "full-blown heroin crisis" in the Green Mountain State.[6]

In his address, Governor Shumlin spoke of the $2 million in heroin and other narcotics that are trafficked every week through his state. Between the years 2000 and 2012, more than 770 cases of treatment for opioid addictions were reported, and 80 percent of the state's inmates were charged with crimes related to drug possession and distribution.

Pressed for a reason as to why a scenic state like Vermont has to grapple with a deadly problem like widespread heroin abuse, the deputy commissioner for drug and alcohol abuse programs for the Department of Health cast a wide net: increasingly progressive attitudes toward drugs (and the risk of even lighter drugs like marijuana playing a role in at-risk populations moving toward more dangerous substances); economic factors contributing to increased access to drugs (whether higher incomes lead to spending on drugs, or lower incomes causing stress and anxiety that lead to drug abuse); even New England's famously bitter winters have been cited as a reason.

However, such questions have been asked time and time again, when rural, tight-knit communities bury another resident and wonder how their quiet little towns became plagued by heroin. The answer is usually the same: No one knows for sure, and there is no single answer as to why heroin is everywhere.[7]

New Battlefields

The problem is such that the opioid epidemic is not just limited to towns and counties in the countryside. The *New York Times* writes that as affluent suburban neighborhoods have banded together to raise awareness of the health risks facing young men and women with bright, promising futures, the tone of the conversation about drugs has changed.[8]

When drug users were "junkies" who lived in crime-ridden inner cities (often in areas with a primary population of people of color), there was a call for being tough on crime and advocating harsh (and, in retrospect, unfair) prison sentences for even the most minor of offenders. But heroin use "skyrocketed among white [demographic groups]," whether those groups are found out in the countryside or living behind white picket fences. In July 2014, the *Journal of the American Psychiatric Association* published the reports of a study that found that over the last 50 years, heroin users are "primarily white men and women in their late 20s," who live outside large cities.[9]

Why the paradigm shift away from the inner cities and to the towns and the suburbs? A May 2016 investigation by the *Los Angeles Times* identifies a pre-existing heroin market, aided by "War on Drugs"-esque policies of zero tolerance toward drug users, and a concerted effort by big pharmaceutical companies to push their opioid-based painkillers on patients desperate to find relief from their chronic pain. When OxyContin became the bestselling prescription medication in America, Purdue Pharma made $31 billion from its manufacture and distribution. This gave the company unlimited leverage in encouraging doctors to continue prescribing the powerful drug, even as it was found to have a shorter timespan of effect than was believed, even as patients reported needing increasing amounts of the drug (or any kind of narcotic to help them manage their pain), and even as bottles of OxyContin could cost hundreds of dollars.

Over a decade, the conditions brewed the epidemic that has killed more than 190,000 people from overdoses on prescription painkillers or illegal opioids (like heroin) when they could not get any more prescription opioids.[10]

Black and White

The director of the White House Office of National Drug Control Policy points out that the demographic that is increasingly being affected by the opioid crisis—namely, white and middle class

Americans—have the resources and connections to call legislators, lean on their insurance companies, and advocate for changes that elevate the tone of the conversation.

The unsaid implications were not lost on African-American advocates, who note that the tone of conversation was markedly different when the overall drug epidemic—be it heroin or crack cocaine—was believed to be a problem that rested with black communities in urban areas. *Valley News* makes the case that entire ethnicities and communities were accused of moral degeneracy when heroin was believed to be a scourge among poor people living in impoverished urban conditions. But when the realization sunk in that opioid addiction (and drug abuse in general) did not respect demographic lines (especially lines drawn by wealthy white Americans living in the suburbs), terms like *mental health* and *treatment* are used in place of *junkie*.[11]

Similarly, *The Atlantic* points out that when drug users were thought to be predominantly black, punishments were often severe. Now that the spread of heroin has changed, and is better understood, the entire context of the situation is looked at in a different light. Or, as *The Atlantic* puts it, "white users made heroin a public health problem."[12]

To that point, *The Economist* writes of how even the popular image of a heroin addict has changed. Three decades ago, the face that came to mind was that of a black male, probably poor, and probably living under a bridge. Today, the face of heroin looks like that of a young grandmother from a suburb in Denver, who got addicted to heroin after developing a dependence on the OxyContin she took following a hip injury.[13]

New Problems and Old Mistakes

But old habits die hard, especially after a generation of misunderstanding and fear-mongering by politicians. Even as white Americans are likely to use "most kinds of illegal drugs," says the *Huffington Post*, it is black Americans who are more likely to be incarcerated for drug offenses.[14] In 2009, the Human Rights Watch reported that African Americans are arrested for drug offences three times as much as white Americans are, even though cocaine use is more prevalent among white communities than among blacks and Latinos (according to a 2011 survey by the Substance Abuse and Mental Health Services Administration).[15]

As explained by Human Rights Watch, and circling back to the point made by *Valley News* and *The Atlantic*, police tend to make more drug-related arrests in low-income neighborhoods, which are typically populated by people of color.

Baltimore, Maryland

The heroin and drug epidemic may have moved out of urban areas and into suburban neighborhoods and rural towns, but the blight remains where it began. In reporting on "the horrific toll" of the epidemic crisis that has devastated America, the BBC writes of how areas laid to waste by crime and poverty are home to users and dealers openly buying and selling heroin and other drugs. In the "subterranean netherworld" of central Chicago, some addicts draw blood as they jam syringes into their muscles, having given up on finding a vein into which they can inject their heroin.[16]

While the small towns of farm country are making headlines as the new frontlines for the opioid epidemic, it is the city of Baltimore, Maryland (the largest city in the state, and with a population of over 620,000 in 2010, the 26th largest city in America) that the US Drug Enforcement Administration says has the highest number of heroin addicts and crime related to heroin in the United States.

Baltimore saw more than 300 deaths caused by heroin overdoses, a year after the American Psychiatric Association's *Psychiatric News* published a study that found that heroin and cocaine were the drugs of choice in urban centers. ABC News called Baltimore "the heroin capital" of the US, as 60,000 people out of a population of 645,000 (or 10 percent of residents) struggle with a heroin addiction.[17, 18]

While the rural areas of the country have environments that contribute to the void that heroin and other opioids are only too happy to fill (low income levels, low education levels, high degree of workplace injuries), Baltimore is infamous for its crime and corruption, its long-simmering racial tensions, and antipathy towards local government and law enforcement. Its strategic location on the East Coast makes it a natural landing zone for dealers to smuggle cocaine and heroin to the other major cities in the region. This contributes to Baltimore's heroin supply being purer, more effective, and much deadlier, than the product that is eventually cut and resold in other big urban locations.[19]

Appetite for Heroin

Such is the extent of Baltimore's heroin problem, where a generation of residents have grown up with "an appetite for heroin," that the city was given the status of a High Intensity Drug Trafficking Area by the federal government. The designation puts federal resources at the disposal of city authorities to hit back against drug dealers as they see fit.[20]

But in a city where a heroin dealer can make $150,000 a day, the drug market is worth at least $165 million. The young African American men selling packets of heroin on street corners don't see that kind of money. With their limited education, they have no job prospects; for many, selling heroin is the only work they can get. It is a vicious cycle that speaks to what the *Baltimore Sun* calls the city's "long-entrenched history" with heroin.[21] It also suggests that even with the federal government's attention on busting the crime rings that have poisoned Baltimore, and hundreds of other cities and communities across the country, it will take a generation (if not more) to turn the tide.

Quoted in the *New York Times*, the chairman of the New Hampshire Governor's Commission on Alcohol and Drug Abuse says that there is no community, demographic, or ethnic group that is immune to the epidemic of drug overdose deaths.[22] Whether in inner cities, affluent suburbs, or distant rural towns, heroin is gradually making its way to the heart of the substance abuse web. Some strands of that web, like MDMA and cocaine, are found in trendy nightclubs and celebrity mansions.[23] Others, like crack cocaine and methamphetamine, might share space with heroin on street corners and rundown low-income housing projects.

But thanks to pharmaceutical companies unleashing a flood of opioid-based painkillers on an unsuspecting (and vulnerable) general public, doctors are more than happy to write prescriptions. As smugglers have learned that some of the most potent drugs are found inside pill bottles at pharmacies, heroin has injected its way into the heart of the drug problem that has corroded urban, suburban, and rural America.

Endnotes

1. "A Small Town Wonders What to Do When Heroin Is 'Everywhere.'" (March 2016). NPR. Accessed May 6, 2016.
2. "Recent Death of Kutztown High Grad Underscores Heroin's Tragic Toll." (November 2014). *Reading Eagle*. Accessed May 6, 2016.
3. "The True Cost of Legalizing Moonshine." (August 2014). *Rice and Bread Magazine*. Accessed May 6, 2016.
4. "Hillbilly Heroin: The Painkiller Abuse Wrecking Lives in West Virginia." (June 2001). *The Guardian*. Accessed May 6, 2016.
5. "America's Pill-popping Capital." (April 2012). *Salon*. Accessed May 6, 2016.
6. "Vermont Gov. Confronts Deadly Heroin Crisis as Public Health Problem." (January 2014). PBS. Accessed May 6, 2016.
7. "Why Vermont Has a Drug Problem." (October 2013). Slate. Accessed May 6, 2016
8. "In Heroin Crisis, White Families Seek Gentler War on Drugs." (October 2015). *The New York Times*. Accessed May 6, 2016.
9. "The Changing Face of Heroin Use in the United States: A Retrospective Analysis of the Past 50 Years." (July 2014). *JAMA Psychiatry*. Accessed May 6, 2016.
10. "'You Want a Description of Hell?' OxyContin's 12-Hour Problem." (May 2016). *Los Angeles Times*. Accessed May 6, 2016.
11. "Column: Changing Perceptions of Heroin Addiction." (May 2014). *Valley News*. Accessed May 6, 2016.
12. "How White Users Made Heroin a Public Health Problem." (August 2015). *The Atlantic*. Accessed May 6, 2016.
13. "The Great American Relapse." (November 2014). *The Economist*. Accessed May 6, 2016.
14. "When It Comes to Illegal Drug Use, White America Does the Crime, Black America Gets The Time."(September 2013). *The Huffington Post*. Accessed May 6, 2016.
15. "Race, Drugs and Law Enforcement in the United States." (June 2009). Human Rights Watch. Accessed May 6, 2016.
16. "The Horrific Toll of America's Heroin 'Epidemic.'" (March 2014). BBC. Accessed May 23, 2015.

17. "Baltimore: The Heroin Capital of the US." (March 2015). *The Fix.* Accessed May 6, 2016.
18. "Abused Substances Differ in Rural, Urban Areas." (September 2012). *Psychiatric News.* Accessed May 6, 2016.
19. "Why Baltimore Blew Up." (May 2015). *Rolling Stone.* Accessed May 6, 2016.
20. "Part 1: Baltimore Is the US Heroin Capital." (n.d.) ABC News. Accessed May 6, 2015.
21. "Heroin Creates Crowded Illicit Economy in Baltimore." (December 2015). *Baltimore Sun.* Accessed May 7, 2016.
22. "How the Epidemic of Drug Overdose Deaths Ripples Across America." (January 2016). *The New York Times.* Accessed May 7, 2016.
23. "Illinois Teen Dies After Taking Drug 'Molly,' Going to Wis. Nightclub." (May 2016). NBC Chicago. Accessed May 7, 2016.

> "Legalizing marijuana could have
> a significant and swift impact as a
> form of criminal justice reform and a
> tool to fight the opioid crisis."

Legalizing Marijuana Is Fundamentally a Racial Justice Issue

Ellen Marks

In the following viewpoint, Ellen Marks argues that even those against marijuana use should back its legalization because enforcement has for many years been meted out unfairly to people of color, particularly in the Midwest. The author adds that the result has been mistrust between law enforcement officials and citizens in inner-city communities that would dissipate if federal laws were adopted that simply legalized marijuana. Such legislation would also allow the government to divert money to fight horrifying drug problems like opioid addiction, notes the author. Ellen Marks is an attorney based in the Midwest.

As you read, consider the following questions:

1. How is marijuana possession prosecuted differently in white communities and communities of color?
2. What does the author propose as a solution?
3. Why is marijuana relatively harmless compared with alcohol, according to the viewpoint?

On Oct. 1, the Marion County Prosecutor's Office announced that it would stop prosecuting minor possession of marijuana charges. It's a good step forward, but it is a temporary, local solution to a national problem, and we need as a country to adopt more comprehensive reform.

MARIJUANA ARRESTS ARE NOT EQUAL

The American Civil Liberties Union said Friday that African-Americans continue to be arrested for marijuana far more than whites in New Jersey, and pushed lawmakers to legalize cannabis before the state legislative session ends in January.

Amol Sinha, executive director of the ACLU in New Jersey, said their analysis showed that black people were three times more likely to be arrested for possession than whites in 2016, despite similar usage.

"Legalization is about racial justice," Sinha said in a call with reporters.

Data from the Federal Bureau of Investigation shows that arrests have increased in recent years, despite growing public support for recreational marijuana. In 2017, New Jersey made more arrests, and at higher rates, than almost every other state. Black people made up a disproportionate share.

A spokesman for the state Attorney General's Office declined comment.

The ACLU's analysis flagged three counties with especially troubling disparities. Black people were six times more likely to be arrested for possessing marijuana in Salem County, and seven times more likely in Ocean, according to the ACLU. In Hunterdon, they were eleven times more likely to be arrested.

Legalizing marijuana is fundamentally a racial justice issue. In June 2013, the ACLU published a study entitled "The War on Marijuana in Black and White: Billions of Dollars Wasted in Racially Biased Arrests." Marijuana possession is heavily prosecuted in communities of color, while enforcement of these laws is negligible in white communities, even though rates of use between blacks and whites are largely the same. In 2010, black users were nearly four times as likely to be arrested as white users. Based on county by county data that the ACLU evaluated, arrest rates in some places were 30 times higher for blacks than for whites. The ACLU report further states:

The racial disparities are as staggering in the Midwest as in the Northeast, in large counties as in small, on city streets as on

The legal weed proposal that fell apart in the state Legislature in March would have also addressed New Jersey's troubled expungement system. Advocates argue that the state should wipe away old marijuana convictions, and direct more money toward communities that have been disproportionally impacted by drug arrests.

Rev. Charles Boyer, a pastor and founder of the civil rights group Salvation and Social Justice, called that comprehensive approach a "moral imperative."

State Senator Declan O'Scanlon, R-Monmouth, released a statement later in the day supporting decriminalizing "small amounts" of marijuana. But he said the issue should ultimately be decided by voters through a ballot initiative, and said he would vote against legalization during the current lame duck session.

State Legislative leaders have previously said they lacked enough "yes" votes in the state Senate.

ACLU's analysis was based on data from the FBI and the US Census' American Community Survey, according to Sarah Fajardo, ACLU-NJ's policy director. She said that while they were only able to track disparities between black and white people, some Latinos may have accidentally been categorized as "white," which meant the disparity could be worse.

"Black People in N.J. Are Still Arrested for Weed More Often Than Whites, ACLU Says," by Blake Nelson, Advance Local Media LLC, November 15, 2019.

country roads, in counties with high median family incomes as in counties with low median family incomes. They exist regardless of whether blacks make up 50% or 5% of a county's overall population. The racial disparities in marijuana arrest rates are ubiquitous; the differences can be found only in their degrees of severity.

These disparities contribute to distrust between police and our communities of color, divert resources that could otherwise be devoted to violent and other crimes, and undermine the very concept of justice.

Consistent with the recommendation of the ACLU, we should legalize marijuana, and license and regulate the production, distribution and possession of marijuana for adults who are 21 and older. And we should expunge the records of those who were convicted of simple marijuana possession so that the adverse consequences of those arrests — from restricted eligibility for public housing to loss of employment opportunities — can be mitigated.

As a country we spend billions of dollars each year on enforcing laws banning marijuana, including court costs and costs of incarceration. The financial and emotional toll on those arrested and their families and communities is far higher. Yet studies find that, contrary to popular belief, the legalization of marijuana reduces violent crime, and based on data from the Netherlands, may even lower the number of users who go on to use more dangerous drugs. Legalization would allow oversight of the supply chain, which would support everything from quality control to taxation.

The history of the treatment of marijuana under US law is rooted in racism (based on its role as the drug of choice for Mexican Americans, Chinese Americans and Black Americans in the early 20th century) and Prohibition-era morality, but it is not based on medical research. There are many good reasons not to use it — it can be addictive, especially when use starts before adulthood; it can have unpleasant side effects; and it can worsen the symptoms of certain psychiatric illnesses, such as schizophrenia. But unlike alcohol, it is virtually impossible to die from a cannabis overdose; it is less addictive and creates less impairment than alcohol; and it has known medical uses, such as pain relief, treating chemotherapy symptoms and reducing seizure risk for those with epilepsy, that are inconsistent with its classification as a Schedule I controlled substance.

Legalizing marijuana could have a significant and swift impact as a form of criminal justice reform and a tool to fight the opioid crisis. We need to stop wasting billions of dollars enforcing laws that cause real harm. It is time to establish prudent regulation of marijuana, similar to the regulation of alcohol, and to end its role in a "war on drugs" that is fundamentally a war on our communities of color. We can and should do better.

> *"The 'policing is racist' discourse is poisonous. It exacerbates anti-cop tensions in minority communities and makes cops unwilling to engage in the proactive policing that can save lives."*

There Is No Epidemic of Racist Police Shootings

Heather Mac Donald

In the following viewpoint, Heather Mac Donald rails against those who claim there is a problem with racial profiling among police officers in the United States and states furthermore that officers confronted by threatening suspects are justified to take deadly measures to defend themselves. Mac Donald also compares and contrasts the actions of African American officers and white officers to support her contention that treatment of white and Black suspects does not indicate prejudice. In fact, the author asserts, the growing perception that racism is rampant among American police officers is quite dangerous. Heather Mac Donald is the Thomas W. Smith fellow at the Manhattan Institute and author of The Diversity Delusion.

"There Is No Epidemic of Racist Police Shootings," by Heather Mac Donald, *National Review*, July 31, 2019. Reprinted by permission.

As you read, consider the following questions:

1. Why does the author claim that lack of minority representation in police forces is not a problem?
2. Why are Democrats targeted for criticism in this viewpoint?
3. Why does the author compare the actions of Black police officers to their white counterparts?

The Democratic presidential candidates have revived the anti-police rhetoric of the Obama years. Joe Biden's criminal-justice plan promises that after his policing reforms, black mothers and fathers will no longer have to fear when their children "[walk] the streets of America"—the threat allegedly coming from cops, not gangbangers. President Barack Obama likewise claimed during the memorial for five Dallas police officers killed by a Black Lives Matter–inspired assassin in July 2016 that black parents were right to fear that their child could be killed by a police officer whenever he "walks out the door." South Bend mayor Pete Buttigieg has said that police shootings of black men won't be solved "until we move policing out from the shadow of systemic racism." Beto O'Rourke claims that the police shoot blacks "solely based on the color of their skin."

A new study published in the *Proceedings of the National Academy of Sciences* demolishes the Democratic narrative regarding race and police shootings, which holds that white officers are engaged in an epidemic of racially biased shootings of black men. It turns out that white officers are no more likely than black or Hispanic officers to shoot black civilians. It is a racial group's rate of violent crime that determines police shootings, not the race of the officer. The more frequently officers encounter violent suspects from any given racial group, the greater the chance that members of that racial group will be shot by a police officer. In fact, if there is a bias in police shootings after crime rates are taken into account, it is against white civilians, the study found.

The authors, faculty at Michigan State University and the University of Maryland at College Park, created a database of 917 officer-involved fatal shootings in 2015 from more than 650 police departments. Fifty-five percent of the victims were white, 27 percent were black, and 19 percent were Hispanic. Between 90 and 95 percent of the civilians shot by officers in 2015 were attacking police or other citizens; 90 percent were armed with a weapon. So-called threat-misperception shootings, in which an officer shoots an unarmed civilian after mistaking a cellphone, say, for a gun, were rare.

Earlier studies have also disproven the idea that white officers are biased in shooting black citizens. The Black Lives Matter narrative has been impervious to the truth, however. Police departments are under enormous political pressure to hire based on race, despite existing efforts to recruit minorities, on the theory that doing so will decrease police shootings of minorities. Buttigieg came under fire from his presidential rivals for not having more black officers on the South Bend force after a white officer killed a black suspect this June. (The officer had responded to a 911 call about a possible car-theft suspect, saw a man leaning into a car, and shot off two rounds after the man threatened him with a knife.) The Obama administration recommended in 2016 that police departments lower their entry standards in order to be able to qualify more minorities for recruitment. Departments had already been deemphasizing written exams or eliminating requirements that recruits have a clean criminal record, but the trend intensified thereafter. The Baltimore Police Department changed its qualifying exam to such an extent that the director of legal instruction in the Baltimore Police Academy complained in 2018 that rookie officers were being let out onto the street with little understanding of the law. Mr. Biden's criminal-justice plan would require police hiring to "mirror the racial diversity" of the local community as a precondition of federal funding.

This effort to increase minority representation will not reduce racial disparities in shootings, concludes the PNAS study, since white officers are not responsible for those disparities; black crime rates are. Moreover, lowered hiring standards risk bad police work and corruption. A 2015 Justice Department study of the Philadelphia Police Department found that black officers were 67 percent more likely than white officers to mistakenly shoot an unarmed black suspect; Hispanic officers were 145 percent more likely than white officers to mistakenly shoot an unarmed black suspect. Whether lowered hiring standards are responsible for those disparities was not addressed.

The persistent belief that we are living through an epidemic of racially biased police shootings is a creation of selective reporting. In 2015, the year the PNAS study addressed, the white victims of fatal police shootings included a 50-year-old suspect in a domestic assault in Tuscaloosa, Ala., who ran at the officer with a spoon; a 28-year-old driver in Des Moines, Iowa, who exited his car and walked quickly toward an officer after a car chase; and a 21-year-old suspect in a grocery-store robbery in Akron, Ohio, who had escaped on a bike and who did not remove his hand from his waistband when ordered to do so. Had any of these victims been black, the media and activists would probably have jumped on their stories and added their names to the roster of victims of police racism. Instead, because they are white, they are unknown.

The "policing is racist" discourse is poisonous. It exacerbates anti-cop tensions in minority communities and makes cops unwilling to engage in the proactive policing that can save lives. Last month, viral videos of pedestrians in Harlem, the Bronx, and Brooklyn assaulting passive New York Police Department officers showed that hostility toward the police in inner-city neighborhoods remains at dangerous levels.

The anti-cop narrative deflects attention away from solving the real criminal-justice problem, which is high rates of black-on-black victimization. Blacks die of homicide at eight times the rate of non-Hispanic whites, overwhelmingly killed not by cops, not by whites, but by other blacks. The Democratic candidates should get their facts straight and address that issue. Until they do, their talk of racial justice will ring hollow.

Periodical and Internet Sources Bibliography

The following articles have been selected to supplement the diverse views presented in this chapter.

American Civil Liberties Union, "Racial Disparities in Sentencing," October 27, 2014. https://www.aclu.org/sites/default/files /assets/141027_iachr_racial_disparities_aclu_submission_0.pdf

Zack Beauchamp, "What the Police Really Believe," Vox, July 7, 2020. https://www.vox.com/policy-and-politics/2020/7/7/21293259 /police-racism-violence-ideology-george-floyd

Jonathan Blanks, "If Someone Disputes Racism in the Criminal Justice System, Show Them This," Cato Institute, September 18, 2018. https://www.cato.org/blog/someone-disputes-racism -criminal-justice-system-show-them

Todd Blodgett, "Stop-and-Frisk Works. Democrats Condemn Legal Practices That Reduce Crime at Their Peril," *Des Moines Register*, February 28, 2020. https://www.desmoinesregister.com/story /opinion/columnists/iowa-view/2020/02/28/stop-and-frisk-legal -effective-democrats-attack-mike-bloomberg/4856378002/

Anna-Leigh Firth, "Most Judges Believe the Criminal Justice System Suffers from Racism," Judges.org, July 14, 2020. https://www .judges.org/news-and-info/most-judges-believe-the-criminal -justice-system-suffers-from-racism/

Michael German, "Hidden in Plain Sight: Racism, White Supremacy, and Far-Right Militancy in Law Enforcement," Brennan Center for Justice, August 27, 2020. https://www.brennancenter.org /our-work/research-reports/hidden-plain-sight-racism-white -supremacy-and-far-right-militancy-law

John Hudak, "Marijuana's Racist History Shows the Need for Comprehensive Drug Reform," Brookings, June 23, 2020. https:// www.brookings.edu/blog/how-we-rise/2020/06/23/marijuanas -racist-history-shows-the-need-for-comprehensive-drug-reform/

Jon Hurdle, "Black People Far More Likely to Be Arrested for Marijuana Possession in NJ, ACLU Study Finds," *NJ Spotlight News*, April 2020. https://www.njspotlight.com/2020/04/black -people-far-more-likely-to-be-arrested-for-marijuana -possession-in-nj-aclu-study-finds/

Toluse Olorunnipa and Griff Witte, "Born with Two Strikes," *The Washington Post*, October 8, 2020. https://www.washingtonpost .com/graphics/2020/national/george-floyd-america/systemic -racism

PBS, "Is the System Really Biased?" *Frontline*. https://www.pbs.org /wgbh/pages/frontline/shows/juvenile/bench/race.html

Ashley Southall and Michael Gold, "Why 'Stop-and-Frisk' Inflamed Black and Hispanic Neighborhoods," *New York Times*, November 17, 2019. https://www.nytimes.com/2019/11/17/nyregion /bloomberg-stop-and-frisk-new-york.html

CHAPTER 4

What Is the Future of Criminal Justice in America?

Chapter Preface

The negative spotlight that shone on the issues of racial disharmony in the United States in 2020, exacerbated by what many considered police murders of Black men and an explosion of both peaceful and violent protest in the streets of cities and towns across the country seems to have precluded any possibility of status quo in the future. People on all sides of the political spectrum voiced the same emotional response: "We can't go on like *this*."

The future of policing and the possibility of greater diversity in law enforcement are the most prominent issues featured in the following chapter. Questions abound. Will a larger number of minority officers create a more peaceful relationship between inner-city citizens and local departments? Will cities and towns across the United States make a concerted effort to hire more minority police officers? Will future cops show equal restraint and compassion to people of color—particularly Black men of all socioeconomic levels—as they do with white people? And will the nation's court system enforce the laws of the nation with fairness to one and all?

Experiments in more creative methods of policing and working with people in poorer, urban communities from a social rather than legal standpoint have begun. The notion of creating safer communities by grooming kids and adolescents to become productive members of society through social services rather than harshly treating them after the die has been cast in gang membership has gained traction in recent years. So has the idea of police officers patrolling alongside psychologists and social workers to prevent confrontation.

What might work for one community might not for another. But most folks feel that something has to change and soon before the next powder keg explodes.

> "Black Americans, and black men in particular, are overrepresented as perpetrators of crime in US news media. This is especially true when looking at the incidence of violent crime."

The News Media Must Stop Spreading Racial Prejudice and Fear

Elizabeth Sun

In the following viewpoint, Elizabeth Sun argues that President Trump and many in the news media have caused panic and exacerbated racism in the United States by pushing false claims about crime. It is imperative, the author maintains, that the media remain unbiased and factual in its reporting. Elizabeth Sun is a student at Columbia Law School and a former Criminal Justice Reform Team intern with the Center for American Progress.

As you read, consider the following questions:

1. How does the media aid President Trump is his politics of fear, according to the viewpoint?
2. What evidence does the author give that violent crime is not as big an issue as the media claims?
3. How much more likely are Black defendants to receive the death penalty compared to white defendants?

"The Dangerous Racialization of Crime in US News Media," by Elizabeth Sun, Center for American Progress, August 29, 2018. Reprinted by permission.

From the start of his presidency, Donald Trump has consistently proven his effectiveness at using fear as a political weapon. At his 2016 inauguration, President Trump claimed that the United States was ridden with poverty and "rampant crime," vowing to put an end to this "American carnage." Since then, he has perpetuated false claims that murder rates are rising overall, even though violent crime rates declined in the nation's largest cities in 2017, continuing the national trend of reduced crime. President Trump has also put unauthorized immigrants at the center of crime by exaggerating the scope and threat of MS-13.

According to new polling by the Center for American Progress and GBA Strategies, this fearmongering works. Eighty-eight percent of survey respondents regarded crime on the national level as either a "major problem" or an "immediate crisis." Meanwhile, only 52 percent felt the same way about their local communities. These levels of fear are inconsistent with national data on crime rates, which has found that both violent and property crime rates have fallen steadily since the 1990s. Furthermore, the drastic 36-percentage-point difference between local and national levels of concern suggests that a disparity exists between how individuals feel in their day-to-day lives and how they view crime in the context of the entire nation. Yet, despite this difference in perception, both national and local media overreport violent crime and are thus considered in this column.

Whether intentionally or not, the news media has amplified national-level fear through its reporting on President Trump. Because national crime perception is an abstract concept, it is likely that the news media plays an outsized role in shaping the public's imagination. Indeed, the news media not only contributes to the public's overestimation of crime through how it reports on the president's controversies, but it also overreports on violent crime— feeding destructive racial and ethnic biases about those responsible.

The Racial and Ethnic Criminal Narrative in US News Media

Black Americans, and black men in particular, are overrepresented as perpetrators of crime in US news media. This is especially true when looking at the incidence of violent crime. For example, one study of late-night news outlets in New York City in 2014 found that the media reported on murder, theft, and assault cases in which black people were suspects at a rate that far outpaced their actual arrest rates for these crimes. The news media also vilifies black people by presenting black crime suspects as more threatening than their white counterparts. It does this in several ways, such as by showing the mug shots of black suspects more frequently than those of white suspects; depicting black suspects in police custody more often; and paying greater attention to cases where the victim is a stranger.

In addition to stoking fear toward black people, the news media worsens racial tensions between black and white people by specifically perpetuating a narrative of white victimization. Homicide, for example, is a largely intraracial crime, but the news media greatly overreports on less common cases of black people committing homicide against white people.

Latinos are similarly maligned in the news media. A study found that 66 percent of the time, news coverage between 1995 and 2004 showed Latinos in the context of either crime or immigration rather than in other contexts. More recent analysis confirms these findings. This treatment of Latinos as criminals and outsiders is especially concerning given that Latinos are otherwise rarely represented in the news media. A recent study found that between 2008 and 2014, stories focused on Latinos and issues concerning Latino communities composed just 0.78 percent of coverage on national evening network news. To put this in perspective, CBS, NBC, ABC, and CNN dedicated an average of just 87 seconds of coverage on Latinos per day—combined—from 2008 to 2014.

In the same way that it overrepresents black people in its coverage of crime, the news media's overrepresentation of Latinos as lawbreakers and outsiders is troubling considering the overall lack of coverage of Latinos. Also, similar to the coverage of black people, coverage of Latinos often speaks in generalities when the story is unfavorable. Positive coverage, meanwhile, is likely to focus on individuals, which allows positive attributes to be seen as the exception, not the rule. In comparison, coverage of white suspects rushes to emphasize the humane aspects of the offender, even in instances when the crime is far more horrendous than a crime committed by blacks or Latinos.

How the News Media Affects Public Opinion

These biases have real-world impacts on public opinion. In a 2012 study, for instance, participants who consumed just one minute of negative news or entertainment on Latinos were much more likely to rate Latinos as unintelligent—even those participants who were disposed to have positive opinions about Latinos at the beginning of the study. The study also found that viewers of Fox News and other conservative talk shows were more likely to hold negative views of Latinos, despite being less likely to know Latinos personally. The result is the criminalization of Latino communities and a negative view of immigration that has led to so-called zero-tolerance policies that are not only ineffective, but also disastrous for those affected.

Biased perceptions of crime can be equally damaging when applied to the criminal justice system. For example, frequent news viewers are more likely to support the use of the death penalty in a hypothetical case, a preference that is dangerous for people of color. A study of Philadelphia, for example, found that black defendants were 3.9 times more likely to receive the death penalty than defendants who committed similar murders. This is most likely due to racialized perceptions of crime, as frequent news viewers are also less likely to believe that black people face structural barriers to success. In addition, public perception of more racial integration is closely linked to greater fear of crime and increased support for punitive measures.

These racialized perceptions play out in the courtroom as well. A study shows that for the same crime, black male offenders receive sentences that are, on average, 19.1 percent longer than those of their white male counterparts. Other studies show that both black and Latino youth are also more likely than white youth to have prosecutors request that they be tried as adults. None of these studies could find a factor other than race—such as the severity of the offense—to explain disparities in prosecutor requests. Thus, racial biases endanger black people and Latinos both inside and outside the criminal justice system—whether through racialized perceptions of crime or unfair sentencing policies.

Conclusion

The news media is an important American institution that is integral to shaping public perception. Purposefully or not, it has unfortunately often spread both fear and racial prejudice, which policymakers have exploited to push through agendas that harm black and Latino communities. Under the Trump administration, it is especially important that the news media look beyond its internal biases and refrain from giving unnecessary publicity to false claims. Only when policymakers and the public have an accurate and data-driven understanding of crime can the United States work toward fair criminal justice policies that are smart on crime.

> *"Atlanta's [police] department stands out as one of the most proportionately representative big city police forces in the nation."*

Opportunity Leads to Diversity in Policing

Beth Schwartzapfel

In the following viewpoint, Beth Schwartzapfel argues that police forces must strive for greater diversity. The author cites the lack of minority hiring of police officers in New York City and the success of Atlanta's police department to create a more diverse force. The author's interview with Atlanta police chief George Turner provides food for thought to those who believe that hiring practices are difficult to change and that finding fully qualified minority candidates is a challenge. Beth Schwartzapfel is a staff writer for the Marshall Project. She has reported on criminal justice issues for such publications as the New York Times *and* Washington Post.

As you read, consider the following questions:

1. What excuse did Bill Bratton give for the lack of diversity on his force?
2. What part does recruitment play for Atlanta's police chief?
3. Why is community policing important?

"Lessons for Bratton on How to Recruit Black Officers," by Beth Schwartzapfel, The Marshall Project, November 6, 2015. Reprinted by permission.

The New York City police commissioner, Bill Bratton, came under fire this week for blaming the lack of diversity in the department on black men themselves: too many of them, he said, have arrest records. "We have a significant population gap among African-American[1] males because so many of them have spent time in jail and, as such, we can't hire them," Bratton said in an interview with the *Guardian* newspaper. (With self-defeating logic, he blamed his own department—with its infamous reliance on stop-and-frisk policing tactics—for creating the widespread arrest records that are his stated obstacle to hiring.)

But at least one American big city offers a challenge to Bratton's claim. Atlanta's population is about 54 percent African-American and 38 percent white. Its police force is 58 percent African-American and 38 percent white. Atlanta's department stands out as one of the most proportionately representative big city police forces in the nation. The leadership of the department—from the chief himself on down—also reflects the city's diversity. The Marshall Project talked to Chief George Turner about how he recruits and maintains a diverse force, why it matters, and why Bratton is just making excuses.

Q: Bill Bratton said that potential African-American recruits in New York City are more likely to have criminal records, and that precludes the department from hiring them. Is that a problem you've run into in your recruitment process?

A: I will just simply say, we have the same recruiting and hiring criteria as Mr. Bratton delineated. We are recruiting from the same base as any city in America. Every year, between four and five thousand applicants apply to be an Atlanta police officer. We hire 200 to 250 police officers a year from that pool. The standards that New York has and all police departments around the country are the same. Young people want to have successes, and they are not going to choose organizations where they don't see an opportunity to succeed.

Q: Tell me about how you built a diverse police force.

A: The conscious leadership in the city of Atlanta made the decision to hire the first eight black police officers in our city in 1948, decades before this happened around the country. I keep a copy of that picture in my office to keep me reminded of the fact that they had to suffer through a lot of challenges to stay in this business. And then the city had to be purposed on recruiting the diversity that represents the city, even back then.

Q: Was that your experience when you began at the Atlanta Police Department?

A: My story is really consistent with what we're doing now. I came on the Atlanta Police Department in 1981. I was attending college at one of our historically black colleges: Clark College, which is now Clark Atlanta University. I was recruited at the end of my junior year. My assistant chief, the second in command, was attending a historically black college probably five years after I came on the department, Morris Brown College, where he was recruited in a very similar fashion.

After I came on the department, you have to develop the leaders that you identify. Once you as a leader determine those young, up-and-coming individuals, you have to develop that talent inside your house. I was a prime example of that. I had an opportunity to be sent back to school to complete a master's degree on the dime of the Police Foundation because someone thought that I had something that might be beneficial in the future for our organization.

When you Google or go onto our website, you see leaders that represent our community. We're deceived if we think young people are not researching us as we're researching them. When they go onto our website and see no diversity in our leadership, they don't see an opportunity there.

Q: Does your department have an edge in that you have a number of historically black colleges you can recruit from in the area? You don't have to ask folks to relocate in order to work for the Atlanta Police Department.

A: If you look at historically black college attendees, they come from all over the country. Young people come down here to go to Morehouse that's from New York. Would a young man that finished Morehouse prefer to police in Atlanta or New York, his hometown? You've got to make the effort. We're not just recruiting inside Atlanta. We recruit throughout the country. We go to cities that are comparable to the urban environment that we're policing. We just returned from Detroit. Cities that are depressed, and that we know that we can get people that are like-minded in an urban setting. It makes sense to those folk that understand the environment we're policing.

Q: When you came on as chief you made a very conscious choice to minimize the use of stop-and-frisk and other wide-net policing techniques. Does that influence the Atlanta Police Department's relationship with communities of color? Does that make recruitment easier in those communities?

A: Some of our tactics that we've gone away from probably has helped our image and the perception that we have in our community. But I'm not under the illusion that we don't have challenges in our minority community, either. We have demonstrations here on a regular basis. But I think the way we handle those demonstrations is really different. We reach out to those organizers, find out what they're trying to accomplish, and try to work with them. I worked on Ambassador Andrew Young's[2] executive protection team when he was our mayor. I learned a tremendous amount from him about strategies that were implemented during the civil rights movement in the '60s. The truth is, we got to where we got because of the leadership of Dr. King and simply having conversations.

Community policing really is about open dialogue between the communities that we have to police in, and coming up with a joint strategy that we have to work collectively to accomplish. The only way you get to that is to know each other. You have to know your communities. We do that by having a good representation of what these communities look like. We are doing active recruiting in the LGBT community. If we could ask the question, what people's sexual orientation would be in this city and in our department, I think we would be really really close to the demographic in that as well. We have two LGBT liaisons that work with that community and keep us in the right direction on where we need to be focusing our attention.

Q: Do you have a message for another big city police chief who says that recruiting a diverse force is really hard?
A: I was on a panel in Phoenix last Friday, and other chiefs asked how challenging it is to recruit a diverse workforce. We don't get a pass as police chiefs when we use that as an excuse. We have to work diligently to change what people see in our departments. And the only way people gauge us is by the officers that are responding to calls.

Q: At a certain point, does recruiting a diverse force become self-perpetuating? Does the applicant pool begin to reflect the city to an extent over time that you no longer actively have to search for a diverse force?
A: The truth is, the best recruiters are our officers. Their friends, their family members. They think the way they think, and they look the way they look. That became one of the best recruiting tools for us. It becomes easier because you have a history.

Endnotes

1. New York City's population is 66 percent non-white; its police force is 45 percent non-white.
2. Andrew Young was a member of the Southern Christian Leadership Conference and a friend of Dr. King's during the civil rights movement. He later served as Ambassador to the United Nations under President Jimmy Carter and then as Atlanta Mayor from 1982-1990.

> *"The most stubborn diversity problem seems to be in the inner-ring suburbs—places where the population has shifted to majority minority, but that are still served mainly by white police."*

Police Departments Have a Hard Time Recruiting African Americans, but Diversity in Police Departments Is Essential

Martin Kaste

In the following viewpoint, Martin Kaste uses interviews with law enforcement officials and African Americans from various areas of the country to argue why creating more diverse police departments has proven difficult. Included among the most prominent reasons are anti-police feelings, disinterest among African Americans in becoming police officers due to low pay, and preferences for other lines of work. Still, recruiters are making the effort to expand Black representation in their departments. Martin Kaste is national desk correspondent for National Public Radio.

As you read, consider the following questions:

1. Why are low police salaries more relevant today than they were years ago, according to the viewpoint?
2. What does it mean to be called an Uncle Tom?
3. Would an influx of black police officers lower tensions in communities beset by gang violence?

Since the Ferguson, Mo., shooting, there have been renewed calls for police departments to hire more minority officers, but it turns out it's not that simple.

Police in the US are more diverse than they were a generation ago. In the 1980s, 1 in 6 officers belonged to an ethnic or racial minority. Now it's about 1 in 4. The challenge these days is finding enough recruits to keep that trend going.

The most stubborn diversity problem seems to be in the inner-ring suburbs—places where the population has shifted to majority minority, but that are still served mainly by white police.

White police such as St. Louis County officer Erich Von Almen.

In the days after the August protests in Ferguson, he and his white colleagues were on patrol in Jennings—a neighboring suburb that's also mostly African-American. He says he understood the outcry for more black officers in communities such as this but that it's easier said than done.

"We can't get more black officers. We recruit predominantly at black schools, the military, and for the life of me I don't know why. It's not the best-paying job; they'd probably do better in the private sector. That's all I can think of. But I know it's not for the lack of trying," he says.

You hear that a lot in America's inner-ring suburbs: Departments say they just can't attract enough minority applicants.

Cedric Alexander, the public safety director in DeKalb County, Ga., got his start in policing and admits that there's something to this complaint. "Many young people today, particularly of color, have far more opportunities" professionally now than 40 years ago, he says.

Alexander got his first police job in the 1970s. Today he's the president of the National Organization of Black Law Enforcement Executives.

"When I first came on, relationships were certainly much more strained—or just as strained—between communities of color and police at that time," he says. But back then, he says, young black people saw joining the police as a way to change things. "And during my generation, that's what we did," he says.

Today, Alexander finds young black people more likely to dismiss the idea of becoming a police officer—but he says that's no excuse to give up on diversity. He says recruiters just have to try harder to win over prospects such as Andrea Dave.

As a black woman, Dave is especially in demand. But even though she's a criminal justice major at Harris-Stowe State, a historically black university in St. Louis, she doesn't sound very excited about joining a police department.

"I mean, if you get into a majority-white police force, you think they're going to be racist. If you get in a majority-black police force, you think they're going to be crooked. It's not really an appealing job anymore like it was when you were younger growing up," she says.

Kevin Minor, a recruitment officer for the St. Louis County Police Department, says anti-police feelings run strongest when he talks to young people in a group.

"Good luck cracking that. Because everybody's playing their role. You got the class clown, you got the 'I don't care,' you got the 'I don't like the police.' You might have one of them that's interested in the career field, but they can't say anything because of peer pressure or whatever," Minor says. When that happens, he says, he tries to catch likely prospects one on one.

The fact that Minor is black doesn't make things easier; he says when he was on crowd control during the Ferguson unrest, black protesters called him an Uncle Tom.

But those feelings aren't universal in the black community. Benny Newsom, also a criminal justice major in St. Louis, says Ferguson didn't sour him on becoming a policeman.

"I think that it kind of enhanced my urge to actually go further in law enforcement," Newsom says.

But he doesn't think diversity by itself will solve the crisis in confidence in the police. "It'd ease the tensions up a bit. But at the same time, they can't be too trigger-happy," Newsom says.

Rather than focusing on being a black officer, Newsom talks about wanting to be part of a new generation of American police—a generation that's more community-oriented and less prone to using force.

> *"He no longer believes that the police can successfully address violent crime on their own. Instead, he's come to see the limits of law enforcement tactics and the importance of the community's role in breaking the cycle of violence."*

A Community-Based Approach Is the Solution

Darwin BondGraham

In the following viewpoint, Darwin BondGraham features Ersie Joyner, creator of the Ceasefire program in Oakland, California. The author argues that imagination and creativity can go a long way to foster healthier and more peaceful relationships between law enforcement and the citizens they are sworn to protect in major American inner cities. BondGraham explains through statistics and an interview with Joyner that the result of the program has been no less than remarkable and can be a shining example for other police departments to seek creative alternatives to archaic and ineffective policing methods. Darwin BondGraham is a reporter on the Guardian's *Guns and Lies in America project.*

As you read, consider the following questions:

1. Why did the old way of trying to eliminate gangs fail, according to the viewpoint?
2. Why has mass incarceration not proven effective in limiting gang warfare in American cities?
3. Why has the Ceasefire program been so effective in curbing gang activity and homicide rates?

E rsie Joyner had a banner year in 1995. He was just four years out of Oakland's police academy when he was awarded a prestigious medal of merit for a seemingly superhuman feat. In one year, he personally made more than 400 arrests. And the evidence room of the Oakland police department (OPD) was crammed with millions of dollars' worth of cocaine and heroin he had confiscated from dealers.

"I thought to myself, I'm on top of my game," said Joyner in a recent interview. "I'm the best of the best."

But looking back, Joyner doesn't see the approach to policing in his early years, and OPD's institutional culture of the 1990s, as effective, or responsible. The aggressive zero-tolerance policies used to lock up thousands of people, mostly for drug crimes, never succeeded in creating a safer city.

"My whole entire career I have been taught, I have trained, and I have worked towards eliminating gangs," said Joyner. "That has failed miserably for us for decades."

Joyner has become a case study in change. Now the head of OPD's Ceasefire program—a successful violence intervention initiative credited with contributing to Oakland's decline in gun homicide rates—he no longer believes that the police can successfully address violent crime on their own. Instead, he's come to see the limits of law enforcement tactics and the importance of the community's role in breaking the cycle of violence in a city like Oakland, which for years was ranked among America's "murder capitals".

Joyner was one of California's top cops in the 1990s. Athletic and street-wise, he grew up in East Oakland and possessed an understanding of the city that few other officers had. He graduated from the elite Bishop O'Dowd private school and studied criminal justice at California State University Hayward. At 22, after only six months on patrol, he was drafted to go undercover in high-risk investigations.

He'd end up spending much of his career there, sometimes working in joint taskforces with federal agencies. Later, he found himself on loan to the FBI and DEA to surveil drug and weapons smugglers who were connecting the Bay Area to the Mexican border. He joined OPD's Swat and the special duties unit, which hounded the armed drug dealers who propelled Oakland's retaliatory cycles of violence.

Wherever he was, Joyner's job always centered on "dismantling" the Bay Area's most violent gangs. And in a police department that prided itself on its reputation for toughness, Joyner, who has a bulldog-like stare, was the personification of the hard-charging cop. He became one of OPD's most highly decorated officers, winning officer of the year in 2002 and taking home six medals of merit throughout his career.

Rising Violence, Tough Tactics

In 1995, the same year Joyner was pinned with his first medal of merit, 140 people were murdered and Oakland had one of the highest homicide rates in the nation. OPD had been policing the city like a wrecking ball, but crime rates remained stubbornly constant.

Homicides had been climbing steadily since the late 1970s, peaking in 1993—the city's deadliest year ever at 165 killings. Black and Latino communities were caught in a vise of unemployment, disinvestment in public infrastructure, a financially tanking school system, and an expensive housing market that locked them out of affluent, whiter suburbs.

How a Pandemic Has Inspired Reform

In the race to curtail the deadly coronavirus, nowhere is the outlook more grim than inside America's correctional facilities. Confinement creates conditions ideal for the spread of any contagion, and the underlying health conditions that can make it impossible to survive COVID-19 are far more prevalent among incarcerated people, as those conditions are among poor and black and brown Americans generally.

So in the midst of a public-health crisis far more frightening than the fear of change, public officials have begun doing what under other conditions would have been dismissed as a reformist's fantasy: dramatically dialing down the punitive machinery of the criminal-justice system. Many police departments have stopped arresting people for lower-level, nonviolent crimes. In Los Angeles County, for example, where the sheriff's department had been arresting an average of 300 people a day, as of mid-March the daily tally had dropped to fewer than 60. Meanwhile, many prosecutors and judges have begun working in lockstep to depopulate jails.

Why it took a pandemic to spark perfectly safe, commonsense restraint in the use of arrest, prosecution and jail is a valid question, but even more important is what police, prosecutors, judges and others in the criminal-justice system will do once the virus subsides — and what the public will demand of them. While government at all levels must invest heavily in the country's recovery and to prepare for other crises to come, how can we continue to dump billions of tax dollars annually into oversized criminal-justice systems that fail to deliver either safety or justice? In what future is it still acceptable for the "justice" system to be a major driver of infectious disease, intergenerational poverty and entrenched inequality?

The stopgap measures we're taking now in the midst of this crisis should push us out of old habits and toward new ones. We not only have to reel in the long arm of the law and soften its force, but our future decisions should also reflect one of the most important lessons in the field: that many so-called criminal-justice problems demand something other than a criminal-justice solution. The path to greater safety and justice for us all runs through communities themselves.

"What a Pandemic Can Teach Us About the Future of Criminal Justice," by Alex Busansky, *Governing*, May 5, 2020.

Murders dropped in the late 1990s as the tech boom swept over the Bay Area, but it wasn't clear the police had anything to do with the improved public safety.

Violence rose again in the early to mid-2000s, without a clear indication of what was fueling the increase. At the time, OPD was doubling down on zero-tolerance tactics under the crime fighting strategy of the then mayor, Jerry Brown. In those years, the Oakland councilmember Larry Reid, who was first elected in 1997 and represents a part of the city sometimes called the "killing fields" because of its high number of homicides, used to ride along with the police on the weekends. Reid had to wear a bulletproof vest.

Reid watched Joyner grow up in the police department. "People have to understand the folks what Ersie and the police were out there dealing with," Reid said. "They were violent. They were not afraid to take a gun and use it, as they are today."

OPD locked up thousands of people and dismantled gang after gang, but they couldn't stop the killing. From 1968 to 2018, an average of 103 people were killed each year in Oakland, according to OPD's data. That's an appalling total of 5,147 lives lost over 50 years in a city of just 400,000 people. Most of the victims were black.

Meanwhile, OPD's tactics came at a price. Large numbers of African Americans were racially profiled, wrongfully stopped, cuffed and arrested, despite little-to-no evidence they had committed a crime. OPD's emphasis on making arrests at all costs often put officers and the public in more dangerous situations.

In 2000, a squad of West Oakland cops who called themselves "The Riders" were exposed for kidnapping and beating up suspects, planting drugs and falsifying reports. Criminal cases against two officers at the center of the scandal, Clarence Mabanag and Jude Siapno, ended in mistrials while another officer, Matthew Hornung, was exonerated. A fourth officer, Francisco Vazquez, fled and remains a fugitive to this day. Juries couldn't agree that the officers were guilty beyond a reasonable doubt, but a separate civil rights lawsuit in federal court brought by 119 black men against The

Riders and OPD proved that their brutal tactics were an outgrowth of the entire department's aggressive crime fighting approach.

The most extreme result of OPD's embrace of zero-tolerance tactics were frequent fatal police shootings. From 2000 to present, OPD officers have been involved in approximately 166 fatal and non-fatal shootings. Joyner has been involved in five shootings, according to department records, and was cleared by internal investigators and the district attorney in each case. Joyner still praises the work of many of his colleagues from that era as "courageous," but he faults the broader strategy that used to guide OPD. "Were we focused on the right thing? Doing police work the way we did it before, we left a huge footprint on the community."

Flip the Switch

For Joyner, there was no moment of epiphany. He says his attitudes about what works to stem violence have evolved over time.

By the early 2000s, the Oakland police were barely treading water with a violent crime rate high above other similar-sized cities, and a continuing lack of trust between the department and people living in neighborhoods most negatively affected by violent crime.

In 2013, Joyner was summoned into the assistant police chief's office in the department's headquarters, a 1960s-era high rise aluminum edifice. The city had been rocked by a particularly violent week, including multiple fatal shootings. The mayor and the police chief were under a lot of pressure to explain to the public how they were going to respond.

The assistant chief told Joyner to take over OPD's Ceasefire program, for years touted by city leaders as Oakland's main anti-violence initiative. OPD had been running the program since 2006, but it wasn't much more than a name. It had gotten sidetracked by budget cuts and competing, and sometimes conflicting, initiatives within the department.

Now, the assistant chief told Joyner to "flip the switch."

"You want me to flip the switch, but you guys haven't paid the PG&E bills, so the lights won't come on," Joyner responded.

The city eventually funded "Ceasefire 2.0," as Joyner calls it.

Today, OPD's Ceasefire 2.0 team works out of offices hidden deep within the department's Eastmont Substation—inside a converted shopping mall where, as a kid, Joyner used to go clothes shopping with his mother. The sides of officers' cubicles display trophy photos of confiscated guns, and on one wall there's the real thing, an AK-47 recovered during a raid and made inoperable, framed like art.

The program is mainly about showing "love and respect" for people at risk of gun violence, said Reygan Cunningham, a former Oakland city staffer who was instrumental in developing Oakland's Ceasefire strategy.

Ceasefire's non-police partners, including not-for-profit groups, clergy and social workers reach out to people who have either recently been suspected of a shooting, or have been targeted in one. Ceasefire team members warn them continuing to engage in violence may lead them to a devastating choice: death or prison. And they offer assistance to help people transition out of whatever situation they're in that is stoking conflicts.

Joyner's squad of officers still conducts investigations and makes arrests when people reject Ceasefire's call to stop the violence. In one recent case, Ceasefire was following four members of an East Oakland gang who called themselves "Playerz Only Live Once"—Polo for short. Polo members were responsible for multiple shootings, had recently murdered someone and shot up a witness's truck when the team developed leads about who the shooters were, and where they could be found. They ended up arresting four suspects, and recovered four guns.

But afterward, Joyner had one of his sergeants go back into the neighborhood, knock on doors, and explain what happened. Hours after he returned to the Eastmont Substation, an elderly woman who lived in the area called to thank him, and she provided one more piece of intel. A Polo gunman had evaded the police and was parked near her home. He had a pistol hidden on the underside of his car. Joyner's team rushed over and arrested him.

The after-operation debrief for the neighborhood has become a regular occurrence—and presents a huge turnaround for a police force that long preferred to operate in secrecy. The policy was suggested by a staffer in the city's human services department as a way to show the community more respect.

The fact that the strategy isn't solely law-enforcement led is partly what makes it successful, according to Ben McBride, a pastor and community leader who was involved with the Ceasefire relaunch. Not that OPD was jumping to give up complete control, McBride noted. During one early meeting, he recalled how a deputy chief in the department asked skeptically, "so you want to have a hug a thug session?"

Joyner's squad has also done away with the illusion that it can, or should "eliminate" gangs. Arresting people, or dismantling their social networks, is the team's last resort.

"The moment we changed our mentality from eliminating gangs to eliminating gang violence, we became awesome," Joyner says.

A Major Breakthrough

The shift is partly tactics, partly economics.

In Oakland, only about 300 people at any given time are responsible for as much as 40% of the shootings, according to researchers who helped launch Oakland's Ceasefire. Many shootings are retaliatory. Over half the city's homicides are the results of running feuds between a relatively small number of groups or gangs. Instead of being driven by competition for turf among street-level drug dealers like in the 1990s, gun violence nowadays often stems from interpersonal feuds that jump from sidewalks to social media.

And many of the shooters aren't the people the police used to stereotype as suspects. For one thing, they're not teenagers. Their average age is 29. The average victim or suspect has already been arrested an average of 10 times. Their risk of killing, or being killed, shouldn't come as a surprise to the police.

Besides, the police department simply doesn't have the resources to go after everyone, Joyner says.

Going on six years, Joyner no longer measures success by the old metrics of arrests made and jail cells filled. Instead, he evaluates Ceasefire's effectiveness through the decline in the number of homicides and non-fatal shootings and the arrests he isn't making.

"We had 68 homicides last year. That is 35 people who did not lose their life who would have in the past," Joyner said.

Non-fatal shootings dropped even more substantially, from 553 in 2012 to 277 in 2018. It's a remarkable change in a city where the pop of random gunfire used to be a common background noise.

"We make less arrests and crime is significantly diminished," Joyner said, crediting the enormous effort of non-police social workers and community leaders in preventing violence.

Starting in 2015, all of OPD underwent a basic training on Ceasefire through its continuing police training program. Joyner thinks getting patrol cops and sergeants leading other units to understand Ceasefire and realize they could contribute to it was a major breakthrough that has made the program a success.

Overcoming OPD's traditional view of policing and convincing officers throughout the department that Ceasefire could only succeed if it responds outside of law enforcement was difficult, he admits.

Many patrol officers saw the Ceasefire team "as a bunch of prima donnas, guys running around in plain clothes and beards driving rental cars thinking they were better than everyone else," he recalled.

"Telling an officer that we have a current identified bad guy who we know is engaged in violence, and instead of putting him in jail—which is what we were taught, bred, and is our natural instinct to do—go out and have a conversation with this person, tell him what we love him, that there are services available for him, ask him to make a change in his life … that was like selling beachfront property on the Mississippi River," Joyner said.

Mcbride and other community leaders remain skeptical of just how much OPD and officers like Joyner have changed. "There's still pressure to take Ceasefire back to the old model of dragnet and suppression policing," he said.

And OPD is still battling enormous internal cultural challenges that continue to fuel a trust gap between many of the city's residents and the police. Black police officers recently accused OPD's recruitment and training division of racially biased hiring practices and unfair promotions. The department's ability to recruit women and black officers is still lagging; currently only 13% of officers are women, and the number of black officers has slowly declined in recent years. In a city where black people make up 28% of the population, just 17% of police officers are black. And OPD recently found that many officers have been underreporting the number of times they've pointed their guns at people, creating faulty statistics and hiding use of force incidents from review.

But OPD, Joyner believes, has turned a corner. "We're not a speedboat. We can't do a turn on a dime. But I feel very confident and very proud of the men and women of OPD who recognize this, who have made this paradigm shift, and more importantly to hold others accountable who don't see it that way."

Periodical and Internet Sources Bibliography

The following articles have been selected to supplement the diverse views presented in this chapter.

Yamiche Alcindor and Nick Penzenstadler, "Police Redouble Efforts to Recruit Diverse Officers," *USA Today*, January 21, 2015. https:// www.usatoday.com/story/news/2015/01/21/police-redoubling -efforts-to-recruit-diverse-officers/21574081/

Deloitte, "The Future of Policing: The Policing Innovations Shaping the Future of Law Enforcement." https://www2.deloitte.com /us/en/pages/public-sector/articles/future-of-policing-and-law -enforcement-technology-innovations.html

Brianna Flavin, "Police Officers Explain Why Diversity in Law Enforcement Matters," Rasmussen College, December 10, 2018. https://www.rasmussen.edu/degrees/justice-studies/blog /diversity-in-law-enforcement/

Connie Hassett-Walker, "George Floyd Death Reflects the Racist Roots of American Policing," The Conversation, June 2, 2020. https://theconversation.com/george-floyds-death-reflects-the -racist-roots-of-american-policing-139805

Joshua Kaplan and Joaquin Sapien, "'No One Took Us Seriously': Black Cops Warned About Racist Capitol Police Officers for Years," ProPublica, January 14, 2021. https://www.propublica .org/article/no-one-took-us-seriously-black-cops-warned-about -racist-capitol-police-officers-for-years

Andrea Lebron, "Examples of Community Policing Strategies at Work," Rave Mobile Safety, April 10, 2019. https://www .ravemobilesafety.com/blog/examples-of-community-policing -strategies-at-work

Brett Pelham, "Are Police Officers Racist? Like the Nature of Racism Itself, the Answer Is Complicated," Society for Personality and Social Psychology, August 31, 2020. https://spsp.org/news-center /blog/pelham-police-officers-racist

Stephan A. Schwartz, "Police Brutality and Racism in America," *Explore*, September-October, Published online July 2, 2020. https://www.ncbi.nlm.nih.gov/pmc/articles/PMC7331505

Scripps National, "Recent Protests Renew Call for More Diversity in Police Departments," The Denver Channel, June 8, 2020. https://www.thedenverchannel.com/news/america-in-crisis/recent-protests-renew-call-for-more-diversity-in-police-departments

Maria Torres-Springer, "The Fight for Equality at the Center of the George Floyd Case," Ford Foundation, June 9, 2020. https://www.fordfoundation.org/just-matters/just-matters/posts/the-fight-for-equality-at-the-center-of-the-george-floyd-case

For Further Discussion

Chapter 1

1. How can cities improve relationships between police officers and citizens while still fighting crime?
2. Should more money be diverted to social programs rather than police departments in communities with gang and crime problems?
3. How big an issue is racism in American law enforcement?

Chapter 2

1. Would legalizing marijuana nationwide help create a fairer criminal justice system?
2. Must the criminal justice system be overhauled to strengthen white collar crime sentencing and bring greater equity?
3. Should the death penalty be abolished?

Chapter 3

1. Can stop-and-frisk laws be carried out without prejudice?
2. Does stop-and-frisk violate the US Constitution, or does it fall in line with suspicion of illegal activity?
3. Are drug laws meted out equitably against those in urban communities as compared to those in suburban and rural areas?

Chapter 4

1. Should city officials work to create better opportunities for inner-city youth to keep them out of gangs?
2. Should equal funding for inner-city public schools be placed into law?
3. Has either major US political party shown a vision for the future in regard to curbing racial discrimination?

Organizations to Contact

The editors have compiled the following list of organizations concerned with the issues debated in this book. The descriptions are derived from materials provided by the organizations. All have publications or information available for interested readers. The list was compiled on the date of publication of the present volume; the information provided here may change. Be aware that many organizations take several weeks or longer to respond to inquiries, so allow as much time as possible.

American Civil Liberties Union (ACLU)

125 Broad Street
18th Floor
New York, NY 10004
(212) 549-2500
email: aclupreferences@aclu.org
website: www.aclu.org

The American Civil Liberties Union uses its resources to fight for and preserve individual rights and freedoms in the United States.

Black Youth Project

5733 South University Avenue
Chicago, IL 60637
(888) 824-4424
email: info@blackyouthproject.com
website: http://blackyouthproject.com

The Black Youth Project is an educational organization intended to strengthen self-expression and knowledge base of African Americans. Among its many focuses are issues involving politics, culture, and gender and sexuality in regard to their effects on Black youth.

Center for American Progress

1333 H Street NW
10th Floor
Washington, DC 20005
(202) 682-1611
website: www.americanprogress.org

The Center for American Progress seeks to improve the lives of all Americans through bold, progressive ideas and concerted action.

Color of Change

1714 Franklin Street
Suite 100-136
Oakland, CA 94612-3409
website: www.colorofchange.org

The Color of Change works to strengthen the lives and power of African Americans by challenging racial injustice, running campaigns that hold police accountable for unfair treatment of Black people, and changing the rules and structure that allow officers to escape accountability for their actions.

Democracy Matters

201 Riverview Drive
Poughkeepsie, NY 12601-3935
(315) 725-4211
website: www.democracymatters.org

Democracy Matters helps students organize projects connecting pro-democracy reforms on such issues as the environment, civil rights, education, and health care. Its goal is to reduce the role of money and increase the role of activists in the American political system.

Dream Corps

436 14th Street
Suite 920
Oakland, CA 94612
website: https://act.thedreamcorps.org

Dream Corps serves to create opportunity for people of color in the United States by lowering the prison population while bringing dignity to their lives and social justice to the country. Its mission is to help create a nation in which the beliefs and cultures of all are respected and individual self-expression is encouraged.

Equal Justice Initiative

122 Commerce Street
Montgomery, AL 36104
(334) 269-1803
email: contact_us@eji.org
website: https://eji.org

The Equal Justice Initiative works to end mass incarceration and excessive punishment throughout the United States. This nonprofit organization serves to challenge the death penalty, as well as racial and economic injustice, thereby protecting human rights for the most vulnerable Americans.

Hip Hop Congress

50 Woodside Road, #203
Redwood City, CA 94061
(213) 215-5257
email: hiphopcongressinc@gmail.com
website: www.hiphopcongress.com

Hip Hop Congress is a network of individuals and organizations seeking to change the world by uplifting culture for the creative development of artists and young people. The organization works to achieve its goals through education, civic engagement, and equitable resource exchange.

Live Free USA

1918 University Avenue
Suite 4A
Berkeley, CA 94704
(510) 295-8652
email: livefree@faithinaction.org
website: http://www.livefreeusa.org/ourcalling

This organization works toward social justice through faith-based institutions. Live Free USA serves to perpetuate policies and practices that will end such societal issues as gun violence and mass incarceration.

New America

740 15th Street NW
Suite 900
Washington, DC 20005
(202) 986-2700
website: https://www.newamerica.org/political-reform/

The political reform program of New America, which began in 2014, looks to launch new strategies and innovations to repair what it perceives as the dysfunction of government, restore citizen trust, and rebuild the promise of American democracy.

Project Mobilize

7674 W. 63rd Street
Summit, IL 60501
website: www.mobilize.org

Project Mobilize is a network of leaders targeting millennials that seeks to create positive change within the system and through existing organizations. It also works to invest in new ideas that would help unify Americans in a progressive manner.

Rock the Vote

1440 G Street NW
Washington, DC 20005
(202) 719-9910
website: www.rockthevote.org

Rock the Vote educates young voters about politics and the election process while encouraging them to become involved at the community level and to vote. The organization has been credited in part for the increased turnout among youth voters in the 2018 midterms.

Bibliography of Books

Tehama Lopez Bunyasi and Candis Watts Smith. *Stay Woke: A People's Guide to Making All Black Lives Matter.* New York, NY: NYU Press, 2019.

Paul Butler. *Chokehold: Policing Black Men.* New York, NY: The New Press, 2019.

Ben Crump. *Open Season: Legalized Genocide of Colored People.* New York, NY: Amistad Press, 2019.

Elliott Currie. *A Peculiar Indifference: The Neglected Toll of Violence on Black America.* New York, NY: Metropolitan Books, 2020.

Angela Davis and Bryan Stevenson. *Policing the Black Man: Arrest, Prosecution, and Imprisonment.* New York, NY: Vintage Books, 2018.

Robin DiAngelo. *White Fragility: Why It's So Hard for White People to Talk About Racism.* Boston, MA: Beacon Press, 2018.

Matthew Horace and Ron Harris. *The Black and the Blue: A Cop Reveals the Crime, Racism, and Injustice in America's Law Enforcement.* New York, NY: Hachette Books, 2018.

Blair Imani. *Making Our Way Home: The Great Migration and the Black American Dream.* New York, NY: Ten Speed Press, 2020.

Ibram X. Kendi. *Stamped from the Beginning: The Definitive History of Racist Ideas in America.* New York, NY: Bold Type Books, 2016.

David M. Kennedy. *Don't Shoot: One Man, a Street Fellowship, and the End of Violence in Inner-City America.* New York, NY: Bloomsbury USA, 2012.

Wesley Lowery. *They Can't Kill Us All.* New York, NY: Back Bay Books, 2017.

Victor M. Rios. *Punished: Policing the Lives of Black and Latino Boys.* New York, NY: NYU Press, 2011.

Richard Rothstein. *The Color of Law: A Forgotten History of How Our Government Segregated America.* New York, NY: Liveright, 2018.

Taleeb Starkes. *Black Lies Matter: Why Lies Matter to the Race Grievance Industry.* CreateSpace Independent Publishing Platform, 2016.

Harriet A. Washington. *A Terrible Thing to Waste: Environmental Racism and Its Assault on the American Mind.* New York, NY: Little Brown Spark, 2020.

Index